ANSWERS

The World's Most Documented Extraterrestrial
Contact Story Continues

STAN ROMANEK

Etherean ™
LLC

Published in the United States by Etherean, LLC, Colorado

This entire story is true and based on actual events.

First Edition
First Printing: January 2012

Publication Data
Stan Romanek
ANSWERS: The World's Most Documented Extraterrestrial Contact Story Continues

1.   ISBN 978-0-9848249-0-8
2.   Unidentified Flying Objects – Sightings and Encounters – New Consciousness – United States – Biography

Printed and bound in the United States of America

Dedication

This book is dedicated to the Human Race and to our off-world friends and guides.

Acknowledgments

To my editor, Ann Diaz, and to my layout person, Carolyn Oakley, I extend my deepest appreciation for your hard work on a short time schedule.

My love and gratitude for the years of friendship and support go out to Mark Stahl, my sister Ann, Heidi Soudani, Victoria Albright, Rick Nelson, Alejandro Rojas, Anna and CJ Locy, Kale Johnson, Clay Roberts, Lucie Blanchard and Lazarus.

For outstanding professionalism and guidance, I'd like to recognize Leo Sprinkle, Ph.D., Claude Swanson, Ph.D., Stanislav O'Jack, Ph.D., and Jack Kasher, Ph.D. Their wisdom gives me strength and reassurance. They have my whole-hearted respect and gratitude.

Many thanks to Jon Sumple, Jack Roth, Sean, Mike, Jamie, and all of the investors for working so hard to complete the documentary of this important story.

A special thank you to my many friends from around the world for the letters, love, encouragement and understanding. Bless you all.

To Mark Leone, thank you for EVERYTHING. You are proof that friends are family you meet along the way. You will forever be in our hearts. The lessons of love, kindness, generosity, forgiveness, understanding and trust will forever be a part of my soul. Thank you, brother.

Saving the best for last: To my wife Lisa, thank you for the endless hours you spend working with me to put our truth into words for the enlightenment of humanity. Thank you for the years of endless support, love, encouragement and laughter. Love you, baby!

Contents

PREFACE 7

1   The Mysterious Woman 9

2   My Search for Answers 18

3   My Posse 22

4   Roadblocks to Finding Truth 27

5   My Story Continues .33

6   From Me to We 51

7   We: the Hybrids 65

8   Regression Therapy .73

9   Predictions 84

10   The Resurrection of Hope 96

11   Discovering My Mission 109

12   Splitting Timelines 121

13   Timeline One 137

14   Timeline Two 144

15   Timeline Three 151

16   The Elaborate Deception 160

17   Children From the Heavens 171

18   Intimidation 182

19   The Return of the Elohim 190

20   Answers: Regression Nine 195

21   The Aztec Conference 216

22   A Last Encounter at the Stanley Hotel 232

EPILOGUE: The End—A New Beginning 248

Preface

In Stan Romanek's first book, *Messages*, we held on to our seats through the wild ride that was his life leading up to the follow-up book, *Answers*.

Along with Stan, we question the strange events, sightings, and encounters that defy our perception of reality and challenge our core beliefs. After all, these things that are happening to him couldn't be real. Could they?

Then Stan presents the evidence to us: the overwhelming mountain of evidence that makes his case the most documented ET experience known. We the readers slowly realize along with Stan that we're not crazy. Not only are we not crazy, but we're actually on the cusp of something really big. We realize that the information coming through is of global and universal significance.

But what is the information? What is the message that lies just outside our awareness?

We get these "answers" in Stan's new book!

I am forever changed from reading *Answers*. I owe a debt of gratitude to Stan for sticking with this mission through unimaginable torment and hardship. He has come out the other side in acceptance of his role in bringing forth this message for humanity.

STAN ROMANEK

His is a message that will resonate with those that are ready to hear it—and infuriate those who are not. The point is that the message is for all of us.

Mark Leone
President
Etherean LLC

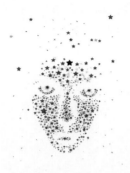

Chapter One

The Mysterious Woman

Southwest of Grand Forks Air Force Base
Northwood, North Dakota
Spring 1968

Kneeling in front of his bright red pedal car, the five-year-old boy was too busy filling the back seat with pebbles to notice the mysterious stranger approaching him from the street. In his imaginative world, he had just discovered diamonds, emeralds, sapphires and rubies in his own backyard, and his thrilling adventure took up all his attention.

He sensed her drawing near before he actually heard her footsteps. When he finally looked up, he saw the tall, pretty woman, walking gracefully toward him. Her feet, it seemed, barely touched the ground. He noticed the way she swung her arms, the way the sunlight framed her blonde hair, her basic navy blue dress.

As she drew closer, her large, slanted almond-shaped eyes captivated him. He had never seen eyes like that before. They were warm, kind, even loving, yet so intense and penetrating that he felt like a frail bird in the presence of a cat staring him down. Her gaze was never distracted from the boy as she crossed the street and made her way into his yard.

He looked around for his mother or anyone he knew to run interference, just in case he had to make a quick getaway, but his mother was in the house. From his spot under the kitchen window, he could hear the clatter of dishes as she was washing up after breakfast.

He turned back around to discover the stranger was right there next to him. She reached down and ruffled his hair. Inexplicably, he felt a rush of affection for the stranger, almost as if he had always known her...as if she were somehow family and a part of his bewildering young existence. He noticed her pale white skin, her long neck and her tapering fingers. Looking up, he thought her eyes as blue as the sky above her.

Mesmerized, he saw a round object suddenly appear in the palm of her right hand. It reflected the sunlight and absorbed his attention. He could feel himself going into some sort of trancelike state as he watched the big blue marble float and spin above her outstretched hand. He also noticed that she only had three fingers and a thumb, and he wondered if she had lost one of her fingers in an accident. Then he noticed that the marble closely resembled a miniature version of the Earth. He knew this because he remembered his mother showing him a globe that his family kept in his brother's room. But what was the Earth doing floating so small in the palm of this strange woman's hand?

"You're a special little boy," the woman said in a reassuring voice. "When you grow up, you'll have something very important to do."

Suddenly, he heard his mother's voice calling his name in a sharp, almost hysterical tone, immediately snapping him out of the trance. He turned and saw her stepping out on to the porch. Turning back to look at the woman, he saw her rapidly disappear down the street corner.

Still in a daze, he could not comprehend his mother's words as she escorted him back into the house. She was grumbling and commenting on the strange woman and was scolding him for some reason.

He did not ask his mother if she had seen the blue marble floating above the woman's upturned hand that was missing a finger. Nor did he ask if she noticed the woman's large, slanted almond-shaped eyes. Like a good son, he quietly walked back into the safety of the house.

Years later, looking back at the vivid details of that event, he often wondered why he had not asked the mysterious stranger some obvious questions:

Who are you?

Where are you from?

Why are you here?

Why do you think I'm special?

How can you hold something without touching it?

Warren Air Force Base
Cheyenne, Wyoming
Winter 1971

Teachers, friends, and family recognized that the boy, now in the third grade, had significant learning problems. But what they didn't know at the time was that his problems were due to his undiagnosed dyslexia. Instead, the Air Force brat at Warren Air Force Base in Cheyenne, Wyoming, was simply considered a slow learner.

The holiday season offered a welcome relief from the taunts, jibes, and insults of his peers as well as the silent judgment of his teachers and the masked sorrow of his parents. With Christmas only a few days away, his family went on a shopping trip at the local Woolworth store.

The day had been long and boring. He had read all his comic books and played with his fuzzy-haired, crewcut G.I. Joe. Now he just wanted to go home. Snow covered the ground, and the icy wind cut through his jacket. He was cold, irritable, hungry and miserable.

Since he was kicking up a fuss, his mother tried to force him back into the two-door Studebaker.

"I don't want to go to another store. I want to go home."

She was pulling the front seat forward when they heard a mellifluous voice.

"You have such a beautiful child," said the voice.

His mother stood up, and the boy turned around to look. There, as tall as his mother, who was almost six foot, stood the mysterious blonde woman looking stately in a long navy blue coat and oversized sunglasses. The boy stuck close by his mother's side.

"Why, thank you," said his mother, a little taken aback. "He's having a temper tantrum," she explained. "If he doesn't stop soon, we may have to give him away."

The woman responded with a warm and enchanting smile. "If you don't want him," she said, "I'll take him." She peered over the tops of her glasses, and even though he was captivated by her sky-blue eyes, he was more focused on the possibility that his mother might just be ready to trade him in.

"Let me think," said his mother, stroking her chin contemplatively. "Hmmm...Oh, I guess we'll keep him." As both women laughed, he climbed into the shelter of the car relieved that his mother was only joking. As the mysterious woman turned to leave, wishing everyone all a happy holiday, the boy couldn't help but wonder where he knew her from.

"What a strange-looking woman," he heard his mother mumble, as she disappeared out of sight.

Ruby Hill Park
Denver, Colorado
Summer 1973

His family property backed into Ruby Hill Park in Denver, Colorado. A winding path linked his neighborhood to the Parks and Recreation pool and playground. Although he was only ten years old, his exceptional athletic abilities had qualified him for the Ruby Hill Park Swim Team.

On this particular day, he had walked up to the pool area a little earlier than practice time. The sky above was a brilliant blue and the air was warm. Denver, a mile above sea level, was enjoying another beautiful summer day. He loved the city and sometimes imagined that the sun was more brilliant here than anywhere else in the United States. At night, the moon appeared closer and the stars much brighter.

While he waited for the rest of the team to arrive, he decided to hang out in the adjacent playground. Lying on his stomach on one of the swing sets, he began his ritual rocking back and forth, watching the ground come up to his nose before disappearing. Content in his fantasy of plunging to great depths below the ocean like a dolphin and then soaring to great heights like an eagle, he did not notice the woman walking up the bicycle path. It was not until she sat on one of the swings close to him that he became aware of her.

He tried to ignore her, treating her with the same reserve he showed toward almost everyone. As she cleared her throat, he quickly glanced up and saw her smiling friendly face. She wore enormous round sunglasses that settled delicately on her small nose.

"Hi," she said, delighted to have caught his attention. "How are you?" Her voice was soft, with a smooth, rhythmic quality.

He lowered his eyes, examining the grains of sand beneath his face while trying to remember where he knew her from.

He did not answer, but instead continued swinging back and forth, his body folded over the seat of the swing, his eyes sweeping over the sand below his face.

"How have you been?"

"Good," he finally mumbled.

"Do you like to play here all by yourself?" she asked.

"I'm waiting for the pool to open," he said. "I'm early for practice."

"So, you like to swim?"

"I'm on the swim team," he said. "We'll practice soon."

"It's early," she said. "You probably skipped breakfast."

"I wasn't hungry," he said.

"You should eat breakfast," she said. "Athletes need to eat well. Sports require lots of energy."

After a long, awkward pause, she spoke again. "You're important," she said. "You're very important. One day, you'll understand. You'll look back on this conversation and feel glad I came."

Startled, he looked up.

She took off her sunglasses and continued speaking, asking questions about his eating and sleeping habits. She spoke to him as if she knew him well, as if she had known him for a very long time, as if she understood all the loneliness and confusion he was experiencing in his young life. But he was more distracted by the magnificent blue-violet color of her unusual, large eyes, trying to recall if he'd ever seen anything like them.

"How are you doing in school?" she asked.

"I hate it," he burst out. "The teachers don't like me and the kids pick on me. Everyone thinks I'm stupid."

"It's not as important as you think right now. When you grow up, they'll discover that you're not stupid at all but extremely smart. Like Einstein, but in a different way. You're very intuitive. You know things without knowing how you know them."

Although his body was bathed in sunlight, goose bumps crawled over his skin.

"Don't worry about what other people think," she continued. "Just remember, you're special. You're part of us and we're part of you. When you grow up, there's something very important for you to do."

Looking up, he stared at her in astonishment: *Why would anyone say such a thing? Especially a stranger, or was she a stranger?* It was at the point that the boy looked up and noticed that she was speaking to him without moving her lips. Startled, he jumped up and ran as fast as he could down the hill flying through the back door and into the protection of his house.

When his mother asked him why he was in such a panic, he incoherently described his experience with the woman who talked to him without ever moving her lips.

"You have to stop making things up," his mother admonished. "It's fine if you don't want to practice."

"But, Mom..."

"You don't have to come up with crazy excuses," she said, irritated.

He did not return for practice and stayed in his bedroom all day. Lying in bed, staring at the ceiling, his thoughts spun in an endless loop.

Nothing made any sense. Worst of all, his own mother didn't believe him. He knew that when his dad came home, he'd be scolded for fibbing. He closed his eyes, pulled the blankets over his shivering body and listened to his heart pounding like a beating drum.

It wasn't until the boy was an adult that he was able to begin putting the pieces together. It was then that he remembered the strange, beautiful woman had first appeared to him when he was five, then again when he was eight, and once more when he was ten.

An artist's rendering of the mystery woman I saw as a child.

How did she know where to find him? Even though his family had moved over and over again, she had always managed to locate him. More than that, how in the world could she hold a marble without touching it, and how could she talk to him without moving her lips?

As you've probably guessed by now, I was that boy, and this is my story. You may find my story unbelievable, which is perfectly understandable. Even now, as a forty-nine-year-old man, I can barely believe it. The woman who had visited me as a child was real—*is* real.

I had a nagging feeling that the mystery woman was somehow connected to the three extraterrestrials who had come knocking on my door, and to me as well. She had said, "You are a part of us—we are a part of you."

My reality bubble had been popped. UFOs are real. Aliens from other planets are real. I had spent many years ridiculing people who believed in such hogwash. My reality was that anyone who believed in such silly fantasies was simply deranged, or just watched too many sci-fi movies. As far as I was concerned, "those people" were just a bunch of Kool-Aid drinking, jumpsuit-wearing weirdoes—until I became one of those people! Suddenly I was consumed with questions about my past—and my future. My tireless search for answers began.

Chapter Two

My Search for Answers

Lakewood, Colorado
Fall 2001

We Are Not Alone

My first abduction terrified me beyond belief. For many weeks I forced myself to believe it had only been a nightmare, nothing more. Only a moron would believe that aliens had actually come to my apartment door, knocked politely, and waited to be let in. Only an idiot would consider the possibility that aliens who looked like possum people would telepathically coo words of comfort such as, "It is all right; you are all right" and then steal you away to do experiments on your body, not to mention fill your mind with mathematical equations, strange symbols, and predictions of the world's future events.

Glimpses of past events had begun to surface—memories of a strange looking woman who had visited me as a child flittered through my mind like mini-movies. I was convinced that I had gone off the deep end. Back in those days, I found an odd comfort in thinking I was crazy because the truth was just too damn scary.

However, this was not a dream. It had happened. I was angry. And I wanted to know why. Why me? What had I done to deserve such punishment?

Lakewood, Colorado
A week later

Making Discoveries

I contacted a prominent UFO organization in Denver on my quest for answers. They helped me to affirm my four recent UFO sightings as well as my abduction experience. I decided to follow their suggestion to go through hypnotic regression.

In my very first experience under hypnotic regression, I was suddenly five years old, then eight, and finally ten. I could see the woman, I could hear her voice in my head, and I could recall every second I had spent in her company. But I still didn't know who she was.

The hypnotic regression experiences were at first very unnerving. Not only did I remember everything that had been done to me, but I also saw it...and felt it. I was once again attached to the wall, connected but not restrained by semi-invisible wires. I noticed that the room was illuminated with a strange bluish light, and could smell a sickly sweet smell that wafted around me. I felt the intense pain as tissue samples were removed from my back. I could hear the Possum Lady cooing words of comfort ("Do not be afraid. It is all right; you will be all right") and recall the consciousness-altering episodes with bizarre writings and equations along with visions of earth-changing disasters that were yet to come. It was as if I was literally back in that strange round room once again.

Most important was the ET's very clear reminder to me: "You are a messenger, you must remember." I laugh now, looking back at this event, just remembering the way she looked at me, like "you poor, slow-witted human." The way she tilted her head, with pity in her huge blue eyes, as if to say, "I can slow this down for you, you poor little earth creature." To this day, at vital and uncanny times, a lot of the information she stuffed into my little brain still leaks out.

Many of my abductions in the years to come were not this polite, nor did the ETs appear concerned about scaring me, or how much pain they were causing. It was like going to work, having a job to do, and being expected to just do it without bitching about the workload. Zetas, or Grey ETs, I have learned, are very emotionless. Being of a hive mentality, they do what they are told and they are very efficient at it.

The encounters continued in the following years, as did my search for answers. We documented it all: the sightings, the equations written on the wall, the broken ribs, the spinning orbs in the yard... Despite my reluctance to play any part in the strangeness I seemed to now be a part of, I was forced to accept that everything I had seen and heard as a child was only the beginning of my journey.

Colorado Springs, Colorado
Fall 2004

Documenting Messages
Understanding and ultimately accepting my role as messenger during those early hypnotic regression sessions, I finally realized that perhaps the Possum Lady was filling my head with visions with good intention. Her predictions of future events would often hit me during the day and completely consume my waking thoughts, at times filling me with such forceful emotions that I would fall into weeping fits, unable to process what my mind was seeing. I worried that I was really going crazy.

No one but my wife, Lisa, knew of these episodes. How could I tell other people about these visions and be taken seriously? I understood people's skepticism, as I'd always had a hard time believing people when they claimed to be able to predict the future. But then again, I didn't believe in UFOs either. If this was real, then maybe it would help to convince me that I had a role to play and that I could somehow help in healing a planet on the brink of chaos. Why else was I given this information? And how could I put it to the test?

At the advice of my good friend and documentary producer Clay Roberts, I wrote down twenty of these predictions and placed them in a large manila envelope along with some important recordings. Clay then sealed the envelope, addressed it to me, and mailed it through the U.S. Postal Office. This is an old practice that people sometimes use to substantiate copyright or proof of ownership of ideas on a certain date (though it doesn't replace having a copyright registered). The concept is that by mailing oneself something and keeping the unopened postmarked envelope, you can prove your date of authorship.

Sure enough, I received the envelope in the mail, tucked it away in my safety deposit box, and promptly forgot all about it. In some sort of therapeutic way, writing down the predictions seemed to allow me to put them out of my mind.

Chapter Three

My Posse

Before we go much further, I need to introduce to you some very important people.

In my book *Messages*, I referred to all of my friends as researchers (though I do have many notable researchers involved in my case, and they, too, have become my friends). My fear of exposing my friends to danger by naming them publicly in my book was my reason for leaving them anonymous. However, that didn't protect them from the events that have transpired over the years. Even still, they have stood beside me through some of the most terrifying events of my life—our lives—sometimes literally looking death in the face and saying, "Bring it on." You will also find these people in my book *The Orion Regressions* as active participants in the session conversations.

These people, along with many that have come and gone, were placed in my life at exactly the moment I needed them. I didn't go looking for them; rather, it was as if we all had a cosmic connection and our paths were destined to cross. Some were to stay, while others were to enter my life, do what needed to be done, and then move on to their next task. Whether they are mentioned in this book or not, they are part of the backbone of my story in a multitude of ways.

Lisa is my best friend, my wife, and the love of my life. My stepkids are April, Nicole (Nicci) and Jacob (Jake). Lisa always has lots to say, so you'll hear from her plenty in my story. When I say "we," I'm usually referring to Lisa and me.

Mark Stahl arrived on the scene early in my life, but we didn't know each other well until later years. He was actually dating my sister while I was still in junior high school! He and I hadn't spoken for years. I moved away and we lost touch until years later when I moved back to Denver to help care for my sister for a time. Shortly before my first UFO sighting, Mark reappeared in my life and we renewed our friendship. He was an active member of the Mutual UFO Network (MUFON) and other UFO organizations, which cracked me up. My best buddy was one of the UFO weirdoes! I teased him about it all the time. He was instrumental in helping me deal with my first sighting, as well as my first abduction. He had connections to help me.

My sister Ann (Nani) helped me as well. In the beginning, I would have lost it—my mind that is—without her and Mark. She continues to be a constant support to me, never doubting that I am a messenger.

After I married Lisa and moved to Nebraska, I met Clay Roberts, a documentary filmmaker from the Denver area. He had heard me on a well-known radio program and contacted me. Clay has since spent years working with me to get my story out. He also provided the surveillance equipment that was installed both in Nebraska and in Colorado Springs, which yielded a lot of video evidence to support my case.

In the two years we spent in hiding from the ETs, whoever was following us in unmarked cars, and anyone who might find out what was happening in our lives, Lisa and I had no friends. When we finally moved to Colorado Springs, Mark and my sister introduced me to Rick Nelson at Mark's **th birthday party. Rick is the founder of the

Paranormal Research Forum (PRF), and he's also involved with MUFON and other amazing organizations that aim to bring public awareness to the reality of ETs and other areas of the paranormal. He is one of my researchers as well as a close friend of the family. After years of solitude and hiding, Lisa and I were thrilled to have Rick in our lives. He introduced us to people who were interested in hearing my story, people who understood me. We were suddenly not in hiding anymore. I had friends and allies. (That's when life got scary.)

A year later we moved out of Colorado Springs, relocating as far as we could feasibly get from that town and the dangers that found us there. We'd been living in our new home for about eight months when we met Alejandro Rojas; Rick introduced us to him after one of my abductions. Alejandro was a MUFON investigator as well as the Public Education Director for MUFON. He became our lead researcher and investigator, with Rick as his backup.

I met Heidi Soudani at one of my talks in Denver, and then again later at another lecture event. We became instant friends. She plays an important part in my life; she too is an abductee.

Heidi and her friend Richard, both real estate agents, spent eight long months working with us to find the perfect home that we could afford. But on top of dealing with us, they had to deal with Audrey, who repeatedly called and told us the house we were looking at had this problem or that issue. Sure enough, the inspectors would come back with that report within days. Finally she gave her approval, and we were home at last. Audrey is a pseudonym for the all-knowing being that calls everyone who helps me. She is polite, direct...and always right!

I met Claude Swanson while he was doing a presentation about his book, *The Synchronized Universe: New Science of the Paranormal* (2003, Poseidia Press), at PRF, Rick's monthly paranormal gathering. Claude is a physicist with a degree from MIT and a Ph.D. from Princeton. He pursued postgraduate work at Princeton and Cornell on the design of superconducting plasma containment vessels for fusion energy systems. He has spent the past four years working with me, figuring out the equations that the ETs put in my head. He, too, became a close family friend.

Next is Lucie Blanchard, a friend I also met through Rick. She lived close to me and provided not only a location to do my regressions, but humor and support close to home. Her only problem is that she blames me for every burnt out light bulb that she's had in the past ten years (a vexing by-product of my ET experiences). Lucie can best be described as a smart-ass character. Hailing from Louisiana, she is a Cajun red pepper. Although she may look somewhat frail, Lucie has a no-nonsense, spitfire rhetoric, spiced with language that would make a sailor blush. Short and slender, she manages to cover a lot of territory, both geographically and metaphysically. In fact, in her younger years, she was known as a powerful exorcist. It was Lucie who suggested I contact Leo Sprinkle.

Dr. R. Leo Sprinkle is an American Counseling Psychologist. He studied at the University of Colorado and earned his Ph.D. at the University of Missouri. Leo came into my life when I was at a crossroads. Either I was crazy, seeing aliens and hearing voices in my head that weren't real, and I needed medication, or I was sane, hearing voices in my head, and seeing aliens that were real. Whatever the case, I knew I needed a psychologist. Leo decided that I wasn't crazy, and then agreed to be my psychologist. He conducted a series of nine regressions that would bring forward a new reality that I had never imagined.

Chuck Zukowski was a volunteer deputy sheriff, a MUFON Star Investigator, UFOnut.com founder, and a researcher of the paranormal, cattle mutilations, UFOs, and the Roswell Crash. He became my friend through Alejandro and Rick. Chuck took on the boring job of being my bodyguard at many conferences, and Lisa's bathroom escort/bodyguard at many of the same conferences.

Stanislav O'Jack studied engineering, architecture, and industrial design at schools such as Eastern Michigan University, University of Michigan, and Cranbrook Academy of Art. He earned an MA in psychology at California State University, a pre-doctorate at the Humanistic Psychology Institute in San Francisco, California, and a doctorate of clinical psychology from the International College in Westwood, California. Stanislav then went on to do his post-doctorate research with physicists William Tiller, Ph.D., and Edwin Young, Ph.D. at Stanford University. Stanislav came into my life as a friend and then as a psychologist, deeming me normal on all fronts.

Jeff Peckman was a politician friend of Rick Nelson's who launched me into the spotlight on a national scale. It was Rick who invited Jeff to one of my talks. He was so blown away by my evidence that he launched the Extraterrestrial Affairs Commission, using my video of the alien in the window to get people's attention and force me to start telling the world my truth.

In the meantime, our circle of friends and allies has continued to grow. People such as CJ and Anna, Nancy, Mark, John (Lazarus), Sal, and Jan all have shared in our stories and experiences, providing keen insights and huge doses of comic relief along the way.

And last, but not least, I'll introduce Victoria Albright. Victoria was a new volunteer for Jeff Peckman's ET Affairs Commission in 2008 when Jeff sent her to my talk in Colorado Springs. If she wanted to see what a real UFO alien abduction case was all about, he told her, that was the place to be. That was our first face-to-face Earth meeting. Imagine my shock when she walked in the door in Colorado Springs. I knew instantly who she was. Six years had passed since I first saw her on an alien craft. That was the night I was put back in a nightgown that didn't belong to anyone I knew. And no, it wasn't hers; I'm still looking for the owner (I want my t-shirt back). I had seen Victoria many times on what seemed to be ships during my abductions; she had few memories of her experiences. As the months turned to years, I can say we have become good friends. What choice did we have? The ETs had ensured we would meet eventually, but even they were surprised we found each other so soon.

So, this is my support group—my posse.

Chapter Four

Roadblocks to Finding Truth

Two Realities

The appearance of the mysterious woman in my childhood made me aware of the existence of two realities existing side by side. It involves the reality of what we believe to be true and the reality that actually exists, which is far grander than anything we have ever imagined. I suddenly had a "knowing" that both of these realities existed within the same space.

Claude Swanson, a distinguished physicist and close friend who helped me comprehend the equations the ETs put in my head, explained to me that Einstein's theories of relativity tell us that space and time are all part of a single physical experience. Einstein called this the space-time continuum. As we physically travel in any direction, we also move in time, going from our past into our future. In essence, space and time are inextricably linked. We can't move through space without traversing time.

The first of our realities, termed the Consensus Reality, is based on what we have been told about our life in the world. It fits into what we consider to be a normal existence. This is a reality that makes sense to us. It is a dynamic reality in which change happens—we meet new people, have new experiences, and mature in our understanding of life. It is a reality where change happens gradually, at a pace we can cope with as it unfolds.

However, there is also another reality, one that is so different from anything familiar that it shatters most of our cherished ideas about how the world should be, and how space-time itself works. This is what I call the Secondary Reality.

In this reality, very little makes sense. Often change is instant and frequently, and, ironically, incomprehensible events are the norm. The mysterious woman in my childhood is a perfect example. She is able to levitate objects, speak telepathically, effortlessly track my movements, and travel from her future to my past.

I have entered this other reality many times. For instance, during a hypnotic regression, I was able to write complex mathematical equations about the physics of space travel with my eyes closed, despite suffering from severe dyslexia, a fifth grade math level, and having zero prior knowledge about theoretical physics, let alone space travel. We finally had some solid proof that the possum lady had indeed implanted that knowledge into my mind.

This Secondary Reality dovetails into the first reality, the familiar Consensus Reality, but it also connects to the stars and the grand scheme of the drama of life.

Those who enter the Secondary Reality feel condemned to a lonely life because they think they are alone in their awareness of it. Most who do hear about it quickly debunk it. This is what my parents did when I told them about my conversation with the mysterious woman who spoke inside my head at the playground. They chose to disbelieve me, preferring to think that I was trying to wriggle out of a swim practice, ignoring the obvious fact that I loved to swim. It didn't fit into their reality. They had been taught to only believe what could be seen with their own eyes. What I had shared with them challenged their worldview, their beliefs. That is part of human nature, much the same as telling someone that red is white, and white is every color of the rainbow mixed together; but the human eye doesn't perceive it that way, so they argue that red is red and white is white, period.

There is resistance to learning anything about the Secondary Reality because it is so bizarre. Here, everything that we so carefully learned about the world around us all of our lives turns out to be far different. We also find our role in the Second Reality may be both humbling and grand.

The Secondary Reality is not an imaginary world. I have huge plastic tubs filled with evidence to prove it. I have videos of spacecrafts and pictures of beings from other worlds. I have plastic medicine vials that were mysteriously melted into globs while sitting in my bathroom cabinet or sitting on the bookshelf in my office. I have Plaster of Paris molds to prove that the footprints outside my living room window were not made by an ordinary human being. Yet, interestingly enough, this world is so strange that despite the mountain of evidence I have accumulated for it over my life, I, too, need help being convincing that it is real.

Good and Evil Forces

Although I was reluctant to accept my mission as a messenger to inform humanity about the reality of extraterrestrial life, I quickly learned that I didn't have a choice. I was consumed with the need to share what I had witnessed and what I was being taught by the ETs. I had a sense of knowing that this was my responsibility, my life's purpose. And as long as I actively told my story, I wasn't taken. If I slacked off, and got lazy, I was abducted. ETs and what I call White Lighters seem to be constantly watching over me and protecting me. They are my invisible guides. However, there are still dark forces—ET and human alike—who don't want me to achieve my goal, and they aren't making my life or my mission easy.

What led me to this assumption was the amount of almost insurmountable obstacles that arose as I attempted to share my story—the message—that we are not alone in the universe.

An opposing force, one with ruthless tenacity and unlimited resources, suddenly showed up in my life, and those representing this force were committed to stopping me. Apparently, talking about the reality of beings far more intelligent and sophisticated than humans threatens national security.

So, who are these elusive people? For the sake of simplification, I call the forces trying to stop me the Black Ops (short for Black Operations). My understanding of the Black Ops is that it is a covert operation involving clandestine activities outside standard police or military protocol. Who they are and what they do is clouded in secrecy because they operate outside the law. In many instances, there are no official records of their operations. There are many people that say there is evidence connecting the Black Ops to the Secret Government, a government behind the official government. The fact that a covert military-industrial government exists has been proven through many documented testimonials from senior congressional members and high-ranking military officers. While most people think of the president of the United States as the head of our country, I've been told that there are many levels of security clearance above even him.

I couldn't have gotten to this point without the help and protection of my invisible allies. Without them, I probably wouldn't be around today to tell you about my experiences. Who are these guardians? They are benevolent ETs and a group of people I call White Lighters: a resistance group within the Black Ops, individuals who have seen through the evil of their own dark organization, and have decided to remain in these positions of secrecy and power as infiltration agents for the good of humanity.

Hidden Agendas

The real question is why would they want to suppress all information about the existence of extraterrestrials? What is this clandestine group trying to hide? For decades people have speculated about the Eisenhower administration's involvement with ETs. There are eyewitness reports online that describe the meeting that the ETs arranged with the president at Edwards Air Force Base in 1954. Many have questioned whether he in fact made a treaty with them. It is my belief that the ETs made an agreement with President Eisenhower and the Secret Government, allowing for the exchange of human DNA for advanced other-world technologies.

So, what happened? Was the treaty broken? Are the powerful elite keeping the information for themselves in order to control society? It's hard to deny there are a lot of realities that someone should explain, such as: Why will 1 in 2 men and 1 in 3 women be diagnosed with cancer, with all of the research and resources available to us (seer.cancer.gov/statfacts)? Why are there 925 million hungry people on our planet (per worldhunger.org)? And why are the rest of us eating genetically modified foods? Why aren't we utilizing free alternative energy solutions that are available (altenergy.org)? There is significant evidence to prove that free energy, new medical solutions, technologies to detoxify our environment, and other revolutionary gains are being kept from the vast majority of the human race.

Facts in the Way of Truth

Why are the Black Ops so intimidated by me and my story? I am one person, one man; how much difference can I make in the world? There are many thousands of abductees, who, like me, are being given information—messages that will benefit humanity. And they aren't being harassed. Today, I understand why.

The ETs have ensured I have validation, proof of my encounters. They've allowed me to take pictures and videos of them. They've allowed me to obtain physical evidence in the form of testable substances such as the implant (which appears to be a bio-nano technology) that was in my hip, materials left in the soil of the crop circles left in my yard, as well as a metallic substance—a mixture of elemental bismuth and beta bismuth trioxide that I somehow swiped from their ship. And they've given me "new physics concepts" to validate that I am getting the information from them. The international success of my book about my abduction experiences, *Messages*, combined with the evidence and veracity of my story makes me a threat to the status quo.

There's lots more. What I discovered about my family's military connection during the 1960s is chilling. More on that later.

Lines of Communication: Introducing Audrey

The synchronicity of the allied forces that protect me, the benevolent ETs and the White Lighters, is amazing and mysterious to me. While I'm unsure as to whether they are working together or separately, it appears likely that the two groups are in contact somehow.

The ETs, apparently following the lead of the White Lighters, found an unusual way to break down the barriers and establish contact and communication with me: via telephone. They use a computer software program that generates a synthesized voice called Audrey. Words are typed in and translated into spoken language.

I used to laugh at the silliness of the whole situation, thinking it was surely some sort of joke or prank to make me look foolish. I mean, come on..."ET phone home" became ET phone Stan. And really, they can speak English? It's a valid question, one that I pondered as well. But then I considered if there really is extraterrestrial life out there and they've found their way here...to my backyard...it's certainly not my place to doubt their ability to pick up a second language.

What wiped the smile off of my face was learning that I wasn't the only one receiving these calls.

It all began with a call from the White Lighters to Clay, the documentary filmmaker I was working with.

Back to my story...

Chapter Five

My Story Continues

Colorado Springs, Colorado
July 2004

The following is a transcription of the message our friend Clay received on his answering machine in July 2004 from the White Lighters:

> Hello, Clay, I apologize for being so forward. It did not take us long to get your phone numbers. Our surveillance is mostly for passive monitoring, but it does come in handy. I cannot tell you who I am for safety reasons, but I can tell you that your perceptions of Stan Romanek and his experiences are real. And, yes, there is a connection with Stan's family and the military but it is anyone's guess what the visitors [ETs] do with Stan. What is important is why they chose him.
>
> As you have probably noticed, Stan is slightly different. The way he thinks, the way he perceives the world, seems to be a little more advanced than usual. His nonverbal communication and abstract thinking skills are off the map. So, yes, he is

slightly different. The interesting thing is that Stan has no idea who he really is. We believe the visitors are going to make a statement, and it will be interesting to see what part Stan will have as this unfolds. There are a few of us in high positions that are tired of the lies. We look to the day when everything will be revealed, knowing it will be enlightening for all. But there are those in specific agencies that would disagree, and for many reasons—most of which have to do with ego and power. And they are getting aggressive because they are scared of the inevitable.

On top of the ET experiences, what Stan has experienced lately is nothing compared to what they will try if he stays in Colorado Springs. Moving to Colorado was a good idea but moving to Colorado Springs is like moving in with the lions. A word of advice: Get them out of Colorado Springs! They should move somewhere less accessible for the military—for their protection.

And staying in the public eye is a good thing. If anything funny were to happen, it would look suspicious, and they do not want to draw attention to themselves. Even with his learning disability—or is it just a different way of thinking—Stan is smart, probably smarter than us. So don't let him fool you with his dumb act.

Stan is doing all the right things but he needs support. Stay focused on your goal but keep an eye out without overly exciting Stan and Lisa. They have a lot to deal with as it is. This has taken a great deal of effort contacting you. So please watch what you say and who you say it to. The immediate people involved in this case are OK, but some of Stan and Lisa's friends are not who they seem!

Clay decided to follow the instructions and didn't tell anyone about it. On the same day that Clay got the White Lighter call, Lisa received a call from someone who hung up after she answered. Using the caller ID, she called the number back and heard a message that sent chills down her spine:

> Welcome to the Public Affairs Office of the Central Intelligence Agency (C.I.A.). If you know the extension of the party you are trying to reach, please dial it now.

Then, two weeks later, we received an Audrey call from the ETs. It was in perfect accord with the message Clay got from the White Lighters:

> Hello, Stan and Lisa. My intention is not to scare or alarm you, but to warn you. It is great that you are back in Colorado, but Colorado Springs was not a good idea. It seems you have moved into their backyard.
>
> Now it is easy for them to get to you. I know how stubborn you are, Starseed, but please heed this warning and know that Lisa and the children are at risk also.
>
> Now listen, Starseed, you know you are different. Follow your instincts and stay alert. This is too important. Soon it will all be revealed, and, Starseed, do not be afraid of what you are.

In a state of shock and consumed with fear that we were being told of danger to the family, I called Clay. It was then that he decided to come clean, and he played the White Lighter-Audrey call recording from his cell phone. In comparing the calls, we realized that the first one told us that they were White Lighters when they said, "There are a few of us in high positions that are tired of the lies. We look to the day when everything will be revealed, knowing it will be enlightening for all. But there are those in specific agencies that would disagree, and for many reasons—most of which have to do with ego and power." While the call I received was definitely from the ETs. The first clue was that they called me Starseed and told me not to be afraid of what I am. The second clue was telling me that I had moved into "their" backyard, and telling me that I had given the Black Ops easy access to me.

It's mind-boggling, to say the least. And I'm still baffled by the whole process. Where are they calling from? How can they contact any telephone on Earth? How can they know everything that is going on? Some of my friends even speculate that they are calling from somewhere off in space itself by usurping our earthly telecommunication technologies. Frankly, I don't pretend to understand how the Audrey communications work; but I do have recordings of many of them, as do all my friends whom Audrey has contacted.

As we were to soon discover, the warnings turned out to be highly accurate. We were paying more attention thanks to Audrey's heads-up call about the danger we were in. Sure enough, the woman and her four children who lived in the house behind us mysteriously packed their bags overnight and disappeared, leaving the yard strewn with her children's toys and the house full of furniture, without so much as a goodbye. Within days of the neighbor leaving, a military woman moved in, and, with alarm, I noticed that she regularly focused what looked to be some sort of surveillance equipment on our house. It seemed that the "they" Audrey had warned us about had actually moved into "our" backyard.

Castle Rock, Colorado
February, 2005

The Fried Van

Once we noticed surveillance from across the back fence, many strange events began to unfold. The story of the fried van is one example.

We were driving back from Denver after conducting an interview for the documentary. After the interview, Lisa and I decided to stop at a fast-food hamburger restaurant on the way home. As we pulled into the drive-thru, a white car pulled up alongside us, stopped, and then drove away. Suddenly the van died and I could not get it to start.

Eventually we were forced to call a friend to come rescue us from the mechanic shop. Four hours later, as we drove up the driveway, I remembered that I'd left all my keys with the mechanic. After checking the front and back doors, Lisa recalled stuffing the garage-door opener in her purse.

"Stan!" Lisa yelled, as she entered the house from the garage.

"What?"

"We just checked all of the doors, and they were locked, but now the front door is standing wide open. Someone must have been in the house. They must have run out the front door while we were pulling into the garage!"

I charged out of the front door to get a glimpse of the intruder, but there was no one in sight.

Frustrated, I returned to the house and immediately checked my filing cabinet. Papers were strewn everywhere, and my worst fears were confirmed: this was no ordinary burglary; someone had stolen all my UFO files...again. Thankfully, after the first burglary, I had made numerous copies and hidden them all over the place.

Then the telephone rang. "Hello?" I answered wearily, almost expecting another death threat from the Black Ops.

"It looks like your van was hit by lightning," he said. "All the circuitry in your van has been fried."

"Lightning?" I exploded. "There was no lightning today."

"Sure looks like it was hit by lightning," he responded defensively.

Suddenly my stepson Jake was yelling. "Stan, someone is messing with the cable!"

"I'll check it in a minute Jake, but it's probably just your T.V.," I yelled up to his bedroom.

"Sorry about that. So, how long will it take to fix the van and how much is it going to cost me?"

"Stan, hurry he's still out there," Jake yelled.

"Damn it. I have to let you go. I'll call you back in a few minutes." Rushing to the sliding glass door, I flung it open and rushed to the cable box attached to the house. Movement near the garage caught my attention; the fence gate door was swinging. Again, no one could be found. We never once considered that the van had been damaged by Black Ops, but anything was possible, and we were damn sure that whoever was breaking into our house, cutting out surveillance camera wires, and other petty harassment was Black Ops. At this point I had braced myself for what might happen next. I was ready for just about anything, or so I thought.

Colorado Springs, Colorado
March 5, 2005

Meeting Grandpa Grey

In my previous book, *Messages*, I talk about my encounter with a small wrinkly Grey we had affectionately named Grandpa Grey. My young stepson, Jake, had some of his friends spending the night at the time, and I'd fallen asleep sitting in my desk chair while working at the computer. A loud noise around midnight awakened me; I opened one eye just in time to see a naked figure running into the kitchen. The first thought that came to mind was that the boys had decided to come up with some outrageous dare. *What a great blackmail opportunity,* I thought, envisioning all the chores I could get Jake to do if I caught him on tape. I quickly grabbed my camcorder and searched the house for the elusive streaker. Try as I might, he was nowhere to be found. I eventually ended up peeking in his room—to my surprise my stepson and all his friends were sound asleep. Baffled, I headed back down the stairs and was about to turn off the camcorder when I spotted it looking at me through the dining room sliding glass door. I can say that I was more than shocked when I realized I was now face to face with what looked to be a small Grey, no more than four feet tall.

A still from the original video of the ET that I videotaped as it watched me from outside our dining room sliding glass door. We affectionately named him Grandpa Grey.

As I watched to see if there might be someone outside somehow controlling a puppet, I noticed the creature's somewhat wrinkly and wizened appearance, as if it were old. To my surprise, it looked as if it smiled and then closed it eyes and slowly moved to the left out of view. Quite scared and dancing around like a terrified monkey, I mustered up enough nerve to run to the kitchen so I could look out the kitchen window in hopes of seeing where this thing went. Unfortunately nothing was in view so I ran back to the dining room, and then back to the kitchen. Still there was nothing. No hidden Black Ops with puppets, no ETs, nothing. It was then I noticed a bright flash. Forty-five minutes later, I woke up on the ground, with no recollection of what happened after the blinding flash. Only after I reviewed the video did I even recall the events of the evening.

The visit from Grandpa Grey remained a mystery. But we were about to find out that *somebody* had an idea about it...and this same somebody appeared to have a hand in our recent van mishap.

Colorado Springs, Colorado
March 11, 2005

Project Romanek
An unexpected document arrived in the mail. It was a copy of a communiqué from the Air Force Space Command, Air Intelligence Agency Division, in Colorado Springs to the Office of Special Investigations (OSI) at the Pentagon—this was from the White Lighters.

On the back was a simple handwritten message, in an elegant script indicating that a female was the sender:

> We have gone to great expense getting this to you. Maybe now you will believe that you must move. Do not release this to the public or contact anyone involved for your safety and ours.

The document was addressed to the commander of OSI, Department of the Air Force, dated February 21, 2005.

Project Romanek:

Be advised, we expect Romanek to have a visitor soon. We will try our best not to miss it this time; there [sic] closeness/ proximity is convenient to say the least. Also HPM worked, van incapacitated. But Mr. Romanek is smart and stubborn and has a strong support system. It also seems that he is getting inside help? We will investigate. If Romanek stays at location HPM can be used on residents and on parties involved, if available? As you know subject must be in range, we will fallow [sic] up as things unfold.

Air Intelligence Agency Division

Shriver AFB, CO 80912-2116

Sincerely,

[name redacted]

"Lisa, this has to be a fake," I said. "It just doesn't make sense. I mean, come on, this is so hokey. Look at this, there is a misspelled word in here. The word *follow* is spelled *fallow,* and it says Space Command? That is so...Star Trek. What I don't understand is how do they know about the van and about visit from Grandpa Grey?"

"I don't know, Honey, but I am going to do some research," Lisa replied. She immediately hopped onto Google and it didn't take long for something to pop up.

"Oh my *gosh*, Stan, listen to this. 'High-power microwave (HPM)/ E-Bomb weapons offer a significant capability against electronic equipment susceptible to damage by transient power surges. This weapon generates a very short, intense energy pulse producing a transient surge of thousands of volts that kills semiconductor devices.

The conventional EMP and HMP weapons can disable non-shielded electronic devices including practically any modern electronic device within the effective range of the weapon. High-power microwave (HPM) sources have been under investigation for several years as potential weapons for a variety of combat, sabotage, and terrorist applications. Due to classification restrictions, details of this work are relatively unknown outside the military community and its contractors. A key point to recognize is the insidious nature of HPM. Due to the gigahertz-band frequencies (4 to 20 GHz) involved, HPM has the capability to penetrate not only radio front-ends, but also the minutest shielding penetrations throughout the equipment. At sufficiently high levels, as discussed, the potential exists for significant damage to devices and circuits.'"[1]

We were not dealing with a fake document. And these people were not just some small-time thugs. We were obviously dealing with an ultra-sophisticated, very well-funded group who used cutting-edge technologies like they were toys.

"Well, that explains why the mechanic was convinced that I had driven through a lightning storm," I concluded.

After sending the document to an investigator that specialized in authenticating government documents (he concluded that the document was authentic), we hid the OSI document and took the warning on the back very seriously. The investigator signed a nondisclosure agreement in order to ensure his silence as well. We didn't take any chances that it would end up on the Internet—public domain. We weren't willing to put the family in danger, nor expose the White Lighter who had helped us understand just how much danger we were in. Despite several more break-ins through the course of the next four years, the document remained hidden and we remained confident that no one would ever see it.

---

[1] http://www.globalsecurity.org/military/systems/munitions/hpm.htm

Northern Colorado
Summer 2009

Our four years of security regarding the document ended the day Lisa received a Google Alert attached to my name. Following the link provided, Lisa went into an angry frenzy. There on her screen was the OSI document. It was located on two separate websites, posted by the same person on both.

Lisa instantly called our lead researcher Alejandro Rojas, in the hope that he could shed some light on the situation. He had no idea how the man who posted it had gotten it. She then contacted not only the blog owner that it was initially linked to, but also the poster, who at the time was the director of the most prestigious UFO organization in the world. The blog owner refused to remove it, but he agreed to remove our current home address, which had also been posted. When Lisa contacted the poster and asked him to please remove it from his personal blog site, he refused as well. Lisa explained that his posting the OSI document had put our family in great danger. He informed her, "I have to disagree with you on that. I didn't put you in danger; Stan did the day he started talking about all of his experiences." And then he hung up on her. In the days to follow, this man began a smear campaign to discredit me, my case, my evidence, and as weird as it sounds, UFOlogy all together.

As if on cue, my avenging angel swooped in and took control of the situation. Audrey decided to take action and send out a clear message: "If you mess with Starseed, we will kick your ass."

Rick Nelson is the founder the Paranormal Research Forum (PRF) and is not only a researcher on our case but also a close friend of the family. Rick received an Audrey call and immediately phoned us and played the recording:

Hello Rick. Regarding Starseed; there are those involved that are not who they seem. We have known this for quite some time. We know who they are and their motives. We allow them to be involved as long as it is a benefit to Starseed. Starseed is correct...the message is for everyone, including those who are against Starseed. When it is time, all that have devious motives, or are [out] to hurt Starseed, will be given a choice to change. If they do not, retribution will be swift and, if necessary, persons involved will be eliminated. Things are changing rapidly. Starseed, along with those that are with Starseed, are protected. But those that would harm, or are against Starseed, will be dealt with. Let this be a warning to those that try to interfere.

At the end of the message, Audrey had mentioned the name of the person who had posted the document. Audrey stated that he would be dealt with. I had no doubts that if Audrey really wanted to do something to this guy, he would metaphorically be dead meat!

And as much as I want to share who was warned, I have received a warning from Audrey as well, reminding me that the message is for everyone and that pointing fingers is not allowed. But she didn't say I couldn't give hints. I'm not scared of Audrey's retribution for giving these hints. I mean, honestly, what will she do to me? Abduct me? I've been there, done that.

The warning in Audrey's call to Rick was reminiscent of her first call to Clay: "The immediate people involved in this case are OK, but some of Stan and Lisa's friends are not who they seem." Many sources have identified a person who is not what they appear to be, and I am confident that this warning was personally issued to that person as well. But we really don't care anymore. We don't dwell on who may or may not be who they seem. Hell, none of us knows who we really are...not yet anyway.

A short time later, I, along with the entire UFO community, was shocked to learn that the director of the most prestigious UFO organization in the world had posted on his blog site that he had resigned his post. Later we would learn the truth was that he had been given an ultimatum: Resign or be publicly removed.

Greenwood Village, Colorado
September 2009

Threats on Our Lives
A few months later, one of my friends received an Audrey call that stated that if I did not stop giving public talks about UFOs, everyone in our little band would be killed in an apparent act of random terrorism on the streets of Denver. A conference at which I was to speak in Denver was coming up: The Galactic Gathering Conference.

It became apparent that the Black Ops found out about this open communication between my team and the ETs. They began to use the computer program Audrey to contact us as well, using the Audrey voice to make us think that it was the ETs, or the White Lighters, calling to warn us. Their terroristic attempts to give us misleading information and warnings via threats proved to be a useless ploy. Initially, however, this ruse worked. They were clever in mixing in concern and information with fear-based warnings.

Although the Audrey calls came from three different sources, we learned, over time, how to distinguish one from the other. We could tell from the quality of the software used, as well as the sarcastic inflections and fluidity of speech, how to tell one caller from another. Usually, the government preferred to use low-tech recordings and create a sense of fear, while the call from the ETs was always calming, even when issuing a warning about something, and it also came with a positive emotional "protective" signature.

After much soul-searching, not to mention working to calm our own overwhelming fear, we decided that the message and the telling of my story was too important to allow them to intimidate us into hiding. We concluded, optimistically, that we must have some pretty good information to share for the good of humanity if it had forced the dark forces to show their murderous intentions so blatantly. I decided to push forward, and all of my friends stood united with me, regardless of the threat to kill us all. We all agreed to attend the conference together in a show of defiance, effectively letting the Black Ops know that we knew they were responsible for the threat, and that we were not intimidated.

However, before the conference took place, my resolve to stand strong against the Black Ops was tested when they decided to send me a personal warning. I had been working in the front yard when I noticed a white Ford Taurus, with no license plates, parked across the street and down about two houses from my house.

At first I didn't think much of it, but wondered why someone would be sitting in a hot car on such a warm day. Then I noticed he was taking pictures of me. I had been a victim of this type of behavior by Black Ops in Colorado Springs, so I didn't hesitate to react. Frustrated and enraged, I stomped my way into the street and headed right for him. When he realized that I was walking in his direction he whipped a U-turn and drove off. My senses were now on high alert, and I kept watch to see if he would return. A short time later he was back, this time parking a little farther down the street. When I noticed the car for the second time, I wondered, *Where the hell do Black Ops find these idiots?* I again stormed out of the house and headed for him. This time, however, he drove right past me, and like a child playing cowboy, shot his finger at me in an attempt to scare me. The rest of the afternoon I kept an eye out for him but didn't see him return.

At about 9 o'clock that night, I decided to take another look down the street to see if the white Ford Taurus had returned. Upon reaching the middle of the street, I looked up and down the block. It was then that I saw a large red orb fly toward me and over the roof of our house. At the moment I turned to watch the orb, I felt something whizzing past my ear. A second later an explosive pop filled the air. "Holy shit! Someone's shooting at me," I screamed, rushing into the house. My stepdaughter April had heard the gunshot, too, and rushed down the stairs from her bedroom just as I ran through the front door.

At the same exact time, our friends Heidi Soudani and Victoria Albright were trying to call our house. Victoria finally managed to get through to warn us that she had received an Audrey call stating that I must stay inside the house. She refused to give Lisa details over the phone, but warned her that it was a matter of life or death—my life or death! The only other information Victoria would share was that Audrey had said, "We have tried many times to reach Starseed, but they (Black Ops) have disrupted the phone lines to ensure that the warning does not reach him. Victoria, please keep trying to get this message to him."

Then, Heidi got through with another warning from Audrey. Heidi's call disclosed that the Black Ops had something sinister planned within the next 48 hours if they could find me alone. I decided to wait until daylight to call the police, as I had no intention of being alone outside the house that night anyway. Lisa pulled all of the blinds, shut off all the lights, locked the doors and sequestered everyone in the downstairs family room. Lisa, Victoria and Heidi worked out a plan to have Victoria come the next evening and spend the night. Because of Lisa's work schedule, her only day off was the following day; after that she wouldn't be able to be home for the remaining duration of the threat.

The next morning, Lisa had to take April, her daughter, to work at 6 a.m. She figured it would be safe to leave me alone for the thirty minutes it would take to get April to work and get back. When she got back I was still asleep but the front door was open. Thinking I was awake, she stormed into the house yelling, "Are you a friggin' idiot, Stan? Do you have a death wish?" When I didn't reply, she checked my office to see if I was there. That's when she saw papers strewn everywhere and that one of my file cabinets had been forced open. In a panic, she rushed to the bedroom where she found me asleep in bed, snoring softly. Returning to the kitchen in the process of checking out the rest of the house, she noticed that the patio door attached to the kitchen was also wide open. She knew it had been closed when she first walked into the house. She screamed. Obviously, the intruder had slipped out while she was checking on me in the bedroom.

That afternoon Victoria called to check in. I told her what had happened that morning and then we began chatting about her recent loss of employment. She had mysteriously been fired after 10 years of working for the same company. The really odd part of it is that she was their top salesperson and hadn't given them cause to let her go. We were speculating whether the Black Ops had something to do with her losing her job, or maybe it was the ETs? Suddenly, her cell phone rang. It was an Audrey call. Grimly, she relayed the message. "The threat window has been extended from 48 hours to 72 hours. I'm heading up right now; I'll see you in a bit," she said.

"OK, drive safe and keep your cell phone handy," I answered.

"Don't worry Stan. I'll be careful. You just stay in the house and away from the windows."

Struggling through those 72 hours taught us the importance of banding together. It appeared the Black Ops were reluctant to do anything in the presence of witnesses, which was fine by me. Audrey had saved my life. If it hadn't been for the orb that flew over the house, I would have been shot in the head. Obviously, the phone lines being blocked had forced them to find a different means of contact, of protection.

Swimming in Chaos

The Audrey communication is not always made by phone. Sometimes messages are delivered as simple environmental beeps that are easy to dismiss. But on July 14, 2005, a series of decidedly non-subtle events began. We saw objects float and watched the faucets randomly turn on and off. Our cats became skittish, behaving like apprehensive warriors in a hostile environment. And we were able to capture photos of what we describe as "shadowlike people."

Someone was clearly trying to gain our attention. We invited a paranormal investigator, recommended by Rick, to investigate.

The investigator prowled around the house with his electronic equipment, which was paradoxically both unnerving and reassuring. After he asked a question into his digital recorder, we heard a drawn-out sound like a groaning ghost. None of us heard it with our own ears; rather, this type of recording is called an Electronic Voice Phenomenon (EVP). We sped up the recording and were amazed to hear the Audrey voice say, "Starseed, it's time."

On another occasion, visiting investigators captured an EVP containing a short conversation between the familiar Audrey voice and a male version of the same voice that would later be used to communicate with us.

"Why are they here?" Audrey asked.

"For Starseed," the male voice replied.

"Can they see or hear us?" she asked.

"Only if we let them," the male replied.

At one point, Lisa and I began to have terrible arguments over the most insignificant things. The smallest things irritated us and we developed explosive tempers. Once again, Audrey intervened, even resorting to calling us in the middle of an argument and telling us to stop fighting. She sees and hears and knows all. The cause of the arguments and emotional upheaval was not a natural cause, such as hormones—the new horror was exposed by Audrey soon after it began.

Apparently, the Black Ops are bombarding our house with satellite surveillance technology, scalar weapons, and delta waves. They can use telephones, computers, audio equipment, and televisions to harass targeted citizens. All four branches of our military have at least one form of PSYOPS, or psychological operations, designed to influence emotions, motives, reasoning and behavior.

But they did not stop at PSYOPS. They also decided to hijack the phone lines when I was on a UFOlogy radio show. In the middle of an interview on Open Minds, hosted by Alejandro Rojas, a deep masculine voice boomed out of the audio system: "You need to keep your mouth shut." The show's engineers were unable to figure out what technology had been used to intercept the broadcast and warned me to stay silent over the airwaves.

Additionally, they have repeatedly placed wiretaps on our telephone lines. When a telephone technician came over to investigate an interruption in our Internet service, he discovered an illegal wiretap at the junction. But the next day, when the technician returned with his supervisor to confirm his suspicions, the tap was gone. Shortly after that incident, we noticed unusual clicks and humming on the phone when we talked. Another tech came to check and found nothing on our hub. But as he traced his way from hub to hub, he found a tap that linked back to our hub—to our line, from another hub in a neighborhood that isn't remotely close to ours.

We've all gotten so used to the chaos that happens to us, this is what normal looks like. And thanks to Audrey's oversight and protection, I am fulfilling my role as a messenger. If we've gone this far, why not further? I, for one, plan to continue to help trigger the shift of awareness necessary to save our planet.

Chapter Six
From Me to We

Northern Colorado
Late Summer 2008

Chest Implant

Early one afternoon as I walked through the kitchen, something outside caught my attention. Above the treetops hovered a silver disc-shaped craft. I flung open the patio door to get a better look. *Oh my gosh, where did I put the camera?* I rushed back into the house, down the stairs, and into my office where I rummaged through the cupboard, grabbed the camera, and ran back to the kitchen door. *Please still be there, please be there.* As soon as I got to the far side of the deck, I snapped a picture of the UFO and zip— it was gone.

The next morning, I woke up and began my day as normal. Decaf coffee, check the news and weather, and then shower. This particular morning, however, I never made it to the shower. As I headed to the kitchen for a second cup of coffee, I felt pain in my right upper chest.

UFO hovering above my neighbor's house the day before I found an implant in my chest.

"What the hell is wrong with me? Lisa, I think I'm having a heart attack or something." As I waited for Lisa to come assist me, I stood rubbing the painful area.

"What is going on, Stan?" Lisa asked.

"I have a bad pain in my chest. Do you think it's a heart attack?"

Between giggles Lisa said, "Honey, your heart is located on the left side of your chest. So unless you really are an alien, I don't think it's a heart attack, Stan."

"Oh yeah, duhh."

"Here, let me pull up your shirt and see your chest...Holy smokes, what happened to you?!"

"What?" I said in near panic. I couldn't see what she was looking at under my shirt. Lisa doesn't usually react like that unless it's pretty bad. "What is it?"

"Well, someone has shaved a fist-sized spot of chest hair off, and you have puncture wounds like when you had the implant in your hip. And the goo has leaked out and attached your shirt to your skin and remaining chest hair. So at least that explains the pain."

I ripped my shirt off over my head to get a look at the damage. "Yeah, but it doesn't explain the implant. I don't remember anything abnormal last night. Wait a minute—yesterday I saw that UFO, but I didn't have any pain then, or when I showered last night."

"Get your camera back out, and let's take pictures," Lisa said.

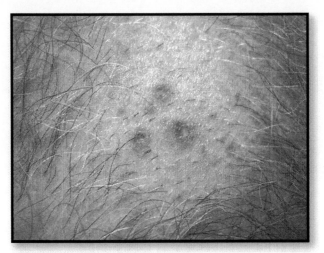

After my wife, Lisa, took this picture, we measured the space between the puncture marks and found it was a perfect triangle.

"Holy crap! Feel this. There's a round thing moving around. Here, give me your hand," I said, positioning Lisa's fingers over the lump in the center of the punctures. "Right there—do you feel that?"

"Yep, that is very odd. Now go get the camera."

"I need to call Rick and the others, so we have to hurry."

"Stan, let me document stuff so we don't forget to do it later."

We set to work taking measurements of the spacing between the puncture marks and the distance from nipple to implant, and took many pictures. Then I finally got away to make my phone calls. I was talking to Rick on the cell phone when I noticed a high pitch squealing was emitted whenever I got the phone in the area of the implant.

Wieeeehheiiweeiihheeeee...

"Stan, what on earth are you doing?" Rick yelled into the phone.

"Oh...sorry, Rick. Did you hear that? It's making the cell phone screech uncontrollably with a feedback loop!"

The next day, I noticed the implant had moved slightly to the right of its original position. At first I thought it was because I could feel it pressing against the skin, so I touched it often to make sure it was still there. I didn't mention it to anyone, figuring they would just make fun of me for "touching myself." The following morning, however, I had to tell Lisa we had to start keeping track of this thing. It had moved another inch overnight. I called Victoria, Heidi, and Rick to let them know what was happening.

The next evening Victoria came to see this thing for herself. By then it had moved across my chest and down slightly and was parallel with my armpit. We took pictures and played connect the dots on my chest, mapping out the path of the implant from the measurement that we previously had taken.

Again at the end of the week, we took a final set of measurements before our planned trip up to Clay's cabin. The implant was located straight across from my sternum, resting on my right rib cage below my armpit.

I was wary of going to the cabin. Every other time that I had been there, I had been abducted. But that was the reason for this trip. I often wonder why I agreed to this wild idea—I should've known better! It felt like I was being offered as some sacrificial lamb.

Clay's Cabin
In the Mountains of Colorado
September 2008

Missing

We arrived at Clay's cabin for a weekend getaway—my wife and I, as well as some of our close friends, Clay, and a few of his friends. Ten people in all. Sixteen if you include the camera crews, who were to document my abduction, if and when it occurred.

In my book Messages, I talk about my past abduction experiences. In the beginning, the ETs focused most of their attention on me, or so it had seemed. But when I tried to make a stand, the ETs went out of their way to prove a point and started involving my stepson, Jake. It forced me to see that the equations I had been writing in my sleep, as well as under regression, were not something I could so easily dismiss, or that I had remembered from a TV program, or that I had stumbled across on the Internet. That's how the ETs work, constantly giving me validation of my experiences, and if need be through other people, either as witnesses or participants. My wife and stepchildren had become involved simply because they were with me. That was a heavy burden to bear. I felt so guilty for exposing them to such terrifying stuff. My wife, also a contactee, tells the story of our family's journey to understanding in her book, *From My Side of the Bed: Pulling Back the Covers on Extraterrestrial Contact—A Spouse's Point of View.*

It quickly became apparent that many people besides me were having these experiences, and, unfortunately for our friends, they too became contactees simply because they were involved with me. This was just the beginning of an understanding that the people who were involved with me had chosen to be—they were supposed to be a part of my life in order to learn through my experiences. And the burden I'd felt for many years began to ease. I wasn't responsible for bringing this to them; they came to me. And we all loved spending time together, sharing stories and just having fun.

Clay arranged for a six-man film crew from Denver TV affiliates CBS, ABC, and FOX to accompany us. They set up surveillance cameras to monitor and capture activity on the deck and surrounding grounds. The entire cabin area felt like the ending scene out of *Close Encounters of the Third Kind,* and we half expected Steven Spielberg to walk through the front door and shout "Action!"

The first night, we all went out on the deck to watch a meteor shower. Sitting on the side of a hill, we had an incredible view of the adjacent mountains and forested area surrounding the property. The deck was an especially good place to watch the show— besides, if anything or anyone tried to sneak up on us, we'd be able to see them coming. As darkness fell, a large but silent flash burst over the top of the woods to the south of the cabin.

"Was that fireworks?" Victoria asked anxiously.

"No," I answered. "I didn't hear any sound."

We stood frozen in place as one flash after another exploded before our eyes, each one closer than the last.

"They're here," I announced.

"Is anyone taking pictures?" shouted a cameraman.

"No, we're all here out on the deck," Heidi shouted back.

"Holy mackerel, did you see that?" yelled another cameraman. "It was like a forty-foot-long tube of light, a foot wide. It appeared out of nowhere and then disappeared."

Several more flashes of bluish-white light erupted around us, but now they were directly above the deck, under the steps, and near the woodpile. The flashes appeared to grow in intensity. A final burst, much like the finale in a July 4th fireworks show, now lit the entire forest around us, accompanied by what I can only describe as some sort of a sonic boom—but much deeper and right next to the cabin. It rattled us all.

Completely losing his composure, one of the cameramen grabbed his equipment, jumped off the deck and ran, crashing through brush, back to the cars. He was so frightened by what had just occurred that he didn't even bother to take his expensive camera off its tripod; instead he just quickly shoved it in his car with the rest of his belongings. In a cloud of dust, he flew like a bat out of hell down the dirt road. Try as they might to stay calm, the rest of the camera crew had also become overwhelmed by all the activity, and by 2:00 a.m. none of the camera crew remained.

Eventually the rest of the group began to grow tired and headed for bed. Heidi, Victoria, and I decided to stay up for a while and talk. Staring at the stars, we couldn't help but wonder who created the light show. We also wondered why they were trying to scare us, and whether they were the UFOs or Black Ops.

Not much later I stumbled off to bed. Heidi and Victoria weren't far behind. Victoria, a light sleeper, decided to stay in the basement bedroom to avoid the rumbling sound of snores that would soon be echoing through the rafters.

During the night, intermittent rustling sounds haunted the cabin. Various members of the group would wake up, grab their flashlights, and look around the room for the mysterious cause, only to find nothing out of the ordinary.

It was still fairly early in the morning, and the sun was just beginning to rise, when I recalled a bizarre dream.

"Lisa, wake up," I whispered. She wouldn't budge.

After rustling the covers in a futile attempt to awaken her, I shuffled off to the bathroom. Upon returning, I dove under the warmth of the covers again, but I had an irresistible urge to tell her about my dream. I leaned on my elbow, staring into her upturned face. I hesitated to wake her for a moment as she breathed gently and looked so peaceful.

"Lisa," I whispered again, more urgently. Her breathing only grew heavier.

"Lisa," I whispered a little louder.

In a smart-aleck tone that only Lisa can accomplish, she mumbled, "Stan, I'm trying to sleep. Go wake up one of your friends."

"They're all asleep," I said.

"Well, so am I," Lisa said, oblivious to the contradiction.

"Come on, please. This is important," I begged.

Her big, beautiful eyes fluttered open. She glanced at the clock and stared at me. "I've only slept four hours and it's not enough," she complained.

"I had the most vivid dream, Lisa. I was outside standing in a field. Victoria was curled in a fetal position in the grass, and I remember that she was wearing white pajamas. I just stood there watching these translucent blue, grapefruit-sized orbs swirling around her."

Lisa was now fully awake. "Are you showing any abduction signs?"

"No. But I don't think it was a dream. Someone needs to go check on Victoria."

"It can wait. Everyone's still sleeping." Unable to drop back to sleep, Lisa finally threw back the covers and grumbled, "I might as well go make coffee."

Instead of donning her robe, she dragged it behind her like a little kid as she headed reluctantly to the kitchen. Lisa banged pans, cups, and utensils around with a deliberate don't-mess-with-me attitude that only she could deliver. If she couldn't sleep in, no one else was going to either. The rest soon began stirring. Even Victoria emerged from the basement.

After talking to our friend Heidi, I decided to go outside and talk to the people on the deck, who by now were all drinking coffee. As I described my dream to them, Victoria was in the kitchen chatting with Heidi.

"The weirdest thing happened," she said. "I woke up with grass all over my bed as if I had slept in the meadow. And my sleeping mask was missing, too. You know I can't sleep without it."

"You should talk to Stan," said Heidi. "He had a dream about this and he thinks it wasn't a dream. He needs to hear this."

Victoria stepped out on the deck. She stood there dressed completely in white pajamas, just like in my dream. After we talked about it, we hurried downstairs to check out her room. A trail of grass led between her bed and the door downstairs. Her sleeping mask lay off in the far corner of her room in the basement.

"V," I said, "I think you've been abducted."

"Everyone, get out," she snapped fearfully. "Lisa, stay here. Search me for any signs. You know better than anyone else what to look for."

The rest of us decided to head outside and look for the spot I had seen in my dream. Although Lisa found nothing unusual on Victoria—no cuts, bruises, or marks—our slumber party crew managed to locate the exact spot I remembered from my dream. The grass was matted in the shape of a curled-up human form.

Things only got worse.

For the rest of the morning, for some strange reason, everyone wore on each other's nerves. Tempers flared, people snapped at each other, and serious arguments broke out. We were all agitated. Lisa, suffering from a pounding headache, said she couldn't take any more bickering and decided to take a nap.

Then suddenly, in an attempt to defuse the mounting situation, and as if guided by some unseen force, we split up into groups of two. Some of us walked around the meadows while others took a short drive into town; Lisa desperately needed a nap, so she stayed back at the cabin.

It seemed as if only a half hour had gone by before everyone returned. Those that had already returned from town were rustling around in the kitchen.

Lisa promptly awoke from her nap and noticed something strange. Once she entered the living room, she began to ask questions. "How long did it take you guys to go to town and get back?" Those who'd gone for a walk said they were out a mere half hour. Others said they had been gone for forty-five minutes. Yet others said they had been gone for an hour.

Always in tune with her surroundings, Lisa glanced over at the clock on the shelf. "That can't be," she objected. "I was only laying down for twenty minutes. How is it possible for all of you to have left at the same time, yet be gone for different length of times, and still show up at the cabin at the same exact time? Something's wrong here."

It was a subtle observation, but she was right. It made no sense.

"Look at the clock," she ordered. "We're missing two hours!"

No one could explain the timeline. There was only one unnerving conclusion: Everyone had been abducted.

Victoria stormed out of the cabin. Everyone else stood around in a state of shock, trying to grasp the unbelievable.

"Everyone, get out here!" screamed Victoria. When we had all gathered around her, she pointed to the ground. "Look."

On the ground, a mere ten feet from the cabin, we could see the telltale sign of a large circle of flattened grass. It looked as if a craft had landed. I had seen markings like this from past abductions.

"Everyone, check someone else for body marks," Victoria instructed. The women searched each other for marks, and their conversation turned quickly to concern over the recent knowledge that Victoria and Heidi were both mothers of hybrid children. This event of missing time made them extra sensitive to whether one of them had just been impregnated, or recently had been, and now no longer was.

Clay checked me over for body marks. He spied a wound under my armpit. "Stan, what's this doing here?" I stared at five fresh gashes on my skin.

"That's where the implant was," I said.

"Check to see if you can still feel it."

"It's gone," I said after pressing around the entire area.

Fear and frustration welled up in me. I'd been taken again. We all had been taken. My mind reeled. Why would they embed an implant and then remove it? Why would they take us all? A strange calm settled over the occupants of the cabin. When most people

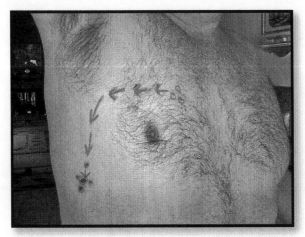

This photo was taken shortly after we realized that we all had missing time. Lisa used lipstick to show how the implant traveled before it was removed.

would be shaking in fear from experiencing missing time and proof of abduction, we were all actually in a jovial mood...except Heidi.

"Heidi, what's wrong. Are you OK?" I asked.

"No Stan, I'm not OK. I just want to be left alone. Please, just don't talk to me right now."

"What's wrong? Why are you crying, Heidi?" I couldn't let her walk away without knowing what had happened. We had all been abducted, and no one else had been affected the way she had. I pulled her into my arms in an attempt to comfort her. I had to know what had happened to upset her so badly. She looked as if she had just lost her best friend. "Shhh," I whispered. "It'll be all right. Just tell me what's wrong."

Through sobs Heidi confessed, "I think I was pregnant. I'm not seeing anyone, so I know that being pregnant is impossible, unless..." Heidi pulled herself out of my embrace and flung herself into one of the deck chairs. She sat silently staring at the mountains. I didn't know what to say to her, how to comfort her. "Stan, I think the ETs had impregnated me again. I think during our two hours of missing time they took more than your implant. They also took the baby."

***

That night, while Lisa and I lay in bed staring up at the ceiling, we discussed our shocking day and I shared Heidi's story with Lisa.

"Do you remember Heidi saying during the last regression that she didn't mind being the donor of offspring up there?" I asked.

"Yes."

"I think this is a lesson for all of us, to be careful what we ask for," I said. "It may have sounded like an exciting idea to be a donor, but it's quite another matter when you are conscious of having been a living incubator and having the baby removed without having any say in it. This whole thing about our not being consciously asked spooks me. I'm not sure if these ETs understand the strong role emotions play in our lives."

In *Messages*, I wrote about an earlier abduction experience when I came across seven children onboard a spacecraft. These hybrid children varied in facial features, and some looked more human than others.

When one of the more humanlike girls wrapped her arms around my leg, I noticed she looked like a young version of me. It was a shock, to say the least, when I then realized that these kids were mine, and that I couldn't save them. During that same abduction, a human woman was sitting beside me. I remembered seeing her during prior abductions. It wouldn't be until years later that I would meet her in person on Earth and learn that she was a surrogate mother of these seven hybrid children on the craft. It was Victoria.

I had recently learned that there were nine hybrid children, seven with Victoria and one with Heidi. Now more than ever I was plagued by the overriding question of why they were using all of us to create hybrid children. Who else was involved in this hybridization program? And who was the mother of the ninth child?

Carney, Nebraska
2003 (a vivid memory)

A Piece of the Puzzle

"Hmm?" I mumbled in my sleep. "Are you OK, Baby?" I asked Lisa, who was sleeping next to me. Did I say that out loud or did I think it? My mind was fuzzy, still half asleep. No response. Perhaps she was dreaming; that's probably what woke me up—Lisa, talking in her sleep. *What the hell was that?* As usual, I was lying on my right side so that I faced Lisa as we slept, allowing me to hold her. It made her feel safe and made me feel equally secure.

As my eyes finally fluttered open, searching for the source of the noise I'd heard from the right side of the bed, I froze in fear. Standing beside Lisa were two Greys, and they were doing something to her.

"Leave her alone, you bastards. Don't you touch her! I will kill you if you touch her. Damn it, stop!"

My scream went unheard. I wasn't able to move my mouth, let alone make a noise of protest, but my mind continued to scream. It was then that I realized I was paralyzed, and it had nothing to do with fear...it was them. I was pissed. Trying with all my strength to move my body—to reach over and pull Lisa into the safety of my arms and beat the hell out of these invasive aliens—was not a possibility. The only part of me that functioned was my mind and my eyes. And then I realized I was getting the same treatment; I too had ETs touching me. *What the hell is going on?* I thought.

My next conscious memory is of waking up on the deck, stark naked, and watching the red blinking UFO from my Old Stone House Park sighting in Lakewood, Colorado—the very same craft I saw before my first abduction with the Possum People—flying away.

After alerting Lisa to my predicament and getting her to once again rescue me from the backyard, we set about the process of documenting the event and eventually climbed back into bed, in the hope of getting a little sleep before the alarm clock went off.

"Lisa, do you remember anything?" I asked.

"No, Stan. I have no memory of anything unusual happening until you woke me up."

"I don't want to scare you, but I remember the ETs doing something to you. I also remember hearing conversations about how appalled they were that humans mutilated their bodies, or something about gynecological removal, but not in those words. It's so hard to explain, but it was as if they had impressed their thoughts into my mind without meaning to do it. All I know is that I got the feeling that they were not happy with you for some reason, and I think it was because of the partial hysterectomy that you had. I vaguely remember hearing, "It makes it more difficult, but not impossible." I have no idea what was going on, but I have a feeling that you were abducted, too..."

It wasn't until years later that I started putting the pieces together. In the spring of 2009, I learned that I had nine hybrid children, and one of them was with my wife.

Chapter Seven

We: the Hybrids

The more I learn, the more I question. Discovering that so many of those around me were either involved or were being pulled in, I began to wonder: *How far back in my family lineage did contact with these ETs really go?*

During a hypnotic regression in January of 2006 with Dr. Leo Sprinkle at my friend Lucie's home, one of the researchers who attended had written out a list of questions for Leo to ask. I share transcriptions of the regression sessions I had done with Leo in my book *The Orion Regressions* (so titled to reflect that most of the information contained in the book came not *from* me but rather *through* me, via an Orion ET—more specifically, a council of three beings from Orion who allowed themselves to be called Grandpa).

This particular segment shows a line of questioning that aimed to uncover details about my family's involvement.

LEO S [Dr. Leo Sprinkle]
GRANDPA [Orion via Stan]

LEO S: ...Thank you. Another series of questions, some about Stan's family. Did Stan's mother play a role in his development?

GRANDPA: Yes. *(Slowly)* Unconscious, unconscious.

LEO S: Unconsciously?

GRANDPA: Yes.

LEO S: Were Stan's grandparents involved?

GRANDPA: No.

LEO S: So the involvement and work with you did not go back beyond his parents?

GRANDPA: Yes. His father...and his mother...his siblings. Stan was... Stan was the right one.

LEO S: Have there been hybrid children created from some of Stan's other family members?

GRANDPA: Yes.

LEO S: Is there information about those hybrid children?

GRANDPA: One. *(Slowly)* Stan's brother...Stan's brother.

LEO S: Stan's brother?

GRANDPA: Yes. Stan's brother, one; Stan, many. Stan's brother one; Stan many.

This small regression snippet reveals that my mother and father had some sort of involvement with the ETs, though it's unclear whether they were consciously aware of it—much the same way I wasn't aware I had fathered hybrid children. I began to search for anyone who could shed some light on how this was possible.

A friend gave me a copy of *Above Black,* a book by former Air Force communications officer Dan Sherman. She felt it could provide some possible explanations. While I currently have no empirical proof for the following hypothesis, I also find it hard to refute.

In *Above Black*, the author talks about a top-secret project run by the Air Force called Project Preserve Destiny. Between 1961 and 1973, certain embryos of military personnel were "genetically managed" while in the womb, giving the offspring abilities that can only be described as enhanced, or beyond human. Electronic intelligence specialists secretly trained to telepathically communicate with extraterrestrials; these communications had to do with military-approved abductions by ETs. I think I was part of this population of genetically enhanced children for several reasons.

For one, I was a military child born in December 1962. For another, I don't look like anyone in my family. But there's more...

My parents' unrelenting attempts to influence me to join the military as a young man has a new significance for me today. I learned through Sherman's book that these genetically altered children generally entered the military to learn how to better use their intuitive communication abilities or psychic abilities.

Learning that "genetic enhancement" is a trait of this select population gives a new perspective on my achievements thus far in life, and serves as further evidence to me that I am of this group. For example, despite my high level of dyslexia, I measure within the genius percentile on intelligence tests. I have a natural aptitude for sports, music, and art. At different times in my life, for instance, I was recognized for being an accomplished recording artist as a Native American flute player, a successful fashion designer whose unusual designs were attracting national attention, and an Olympic hopeful track cyclist who competed with some of the best in the world. And now that I've started to open up about my experiences, I get to add "international bestselling author" to that list—it's all pretty incredible and I don't take it for granted.

Since my first abduction, I also seem to have gained some slight extra-sensory abilities, both mentally and physically. In what I call spontaneous knowingness, I am able to envision or understand a problem or set of circumstances in a most profound way—far beyond what we normally refer to as intuition. I also am able to physically feel other people's pain when I get near them, and can often alleviate the pain they are experiencing by touching them. My hands get exceptionally hot, as if energy from some other source is working through me.

Is this all just sheer coincidence, or did my father keep crucial information from me? Or, is my father altogether blissfully unaware of the part he played?

The Mystery Woman

When the mysterious lady first showed up in my life in 1968 in Northwood, North Dakota, a UFO was seen in that city during that time, just after it appeared at military installations at Minot and then Grand Forks Air Force Base where my father worked. After the UFO was seen hovering above the water tower in our small town of Northwood, my parents did something unusual in those days—they began to purchase bottled water.

I suspect that my father's reticence to talk about his past is much more than fear of upsetting his former military bosses. It runs deeper. During my father's years in the military he was transferred quite often. We relocated from North Dakota to Wyoming and then finally back to Colorado where I was born. After working at the nuclear missile silos he was stationed at Lowry Air Force Base. I would later learn that my mother was employed at Rocky Flats, a top-secret site for nuclear experiments production and nuclear waste disposal. My parents were always secretive about their work, but I suspected that they had top-secret clearance and extensive military connections. As time passed and after many experiences, I often wondered whether there was a link between my parent's clandestine careers and the mysterious woman.

Further Revelations

In 2010, I was approached by the son of a general who had been in charge of the nuclear silo bases during the time my father was stationed at Grand Forks Air Force Base in North Dakota. He explained to me that his father's assignments had included supervision of Minot and Grand Forks Air Force Bases, and, because his father was terminally ill, he had revealed to him the ET contact with the silos! I asked the son why the general didn't reveal this at the National Press Club UFO Conference on September 29, 2010, as many other brave military personnel did. He said they'd never heard of the conference, and that his father was too sick to travel. I expressed my condolences and then asked why he contacted me. I was told that the general had proof that UFOs had hovered over nuclear silos between 1966 and 1968 and disabled the nuclear missiles. What's more, a second report in his possession discloses that a UFO had actually landed near a missile silo in North Dakota.

What was revealed, also, was the enormity of the visitation. The ETs chose to activate and arm a nuclear missile without the required presidential codes at the very bases where my own father was working. This stirred a national crisis among military intelligence. The implications were profound: The security of the entire military nuclear program of the United States had become obsolete overnight.

These events occurred around the same time that I had my first visit from the strange, beautiful mystery woman.

The general's son also had documents and photos of this entire incident in his possession. Today, more than 120 documents around these silo incidents have been placed in my possession. I'll include only a few pages of these documents here for relevancy, and will release the rest of the documents when the time's right.

After receiving this evidence, I consulted with military personnel to see if these documents were valid. They pointed out that the documentation uses military jargon typical for that time. The ranks mentioned also existed only at that time. For instance, ranks of Airman Second Class and Airman Third Class appear in some of the documents although those ranks no longer exist. Misspellings are also typical for that time because most military personnel did not have college degrees; since that was around the height of the Vietnam War, able-bodied and young was all a soldier needed to be.

All the records in my possession come under President Clinton's April 1995 Executive Order 12958, which provides for automatic declassification of classified documents more than twenty-five years old. Once declassified, a government document enters the public domain. These documents prove our government has been involved in a long-term cover-up of extraterrestrial contact. It's now a documented fact that UFOs appeared at Minot AFB, Grand Forks AFB, and bases in Montana. Names and eyewitness accounts are cited in the official reports.

This picture was included with the 120 documents that I received. The photo was taken by Military Police as the UFO was tracked to Grand Forks AFB.

TOP SECRET

USAFE 68   TT I72{   TOP SECRET   6 June 1968

From IO OB

6 June 1968, 1440 hours. Duration 22-mins.
South West of Minot North Dakota.

    Sergeant on duty got a call from MP  He stated that
the guards at one of the missile silos come over to see a strange object
fly in over a silo. Sergeant ███████took two other men with him to
check-in. Arriving at the gate of the silo Sergeant ███████ noticed that
the guards at the silo were like statues and the locks on the gates were
open. The sergeant then had contact with the officers down in the silo.
They were very upset and stated that the missile had been armed and
unlocked in launch mode, and that the warhead was armed.

    The object was apparently simultaneously tract by radar and
headed east to Grand Forks then South West .-

TOP   SECRET

(END OF USAFE ITEM 68)

████████████████

2 of 5

*Above is one of 120 documents I received from the son of a general who
was involved with the same missile bases where my father worked in the
late 1960s. This document serves as evidence that a UFO armed a missile
at Minot AFB.*

Ironically, my father refuses to talk about it—despite the official documents I've shown him, despite the success of my book *Messages*, and despite my confronting him about conversations I overheard in the house when I was a boy.

Why did this event correspond with my first meeting with the strange woman? Why was I visited so often as a child? What was the purpose of introducing me to this strange looking woman? Why have I been abducted at least twelve times, from my mid-thirties until the present age of forty-nine? It is almost as if the ETs are monitoring my progress as an adult since I had refused to join the military. Maybe the ETs who were involved got wise to the fact that the government was using the hybrid-humans to do more than communicate telepathically; maybe some of these genetically altered children were being used as weapons against the ETs. Who knows? It's a possibility. Maybe that's why I am of such great interest. I had said "Hell no" to the military and to my parents and followed my own path.

I was seventeen when I left home and struck out into the world on my own. At that time, I wasn't thinking at all about the mysterious woman who had visited me several times as a child. I'd all but forgotten about how disturbed I was by her ability to read my mind, her unusual slanted sky-blue eyes and three-fingered hands, and her ability to float objects midair. In retrospect I can see that she intended well, but as a child, I was not able to appreciate her loving disposition, sympathetic words, and affectionate concern for my welfare. Many years would pass before I would learn who this mystery woman from my childhood was—who she is.

Chapter Eight

Regression Therapy

Trying to understand my experiences with my children from the heavens was not an easy thing. It was as if I were living in two completely different but parallel worlds. In one world, my primary reality, the conventions and beliefs I grew up with made perfect sense. This was the world of everyday living. But there was also this other world, which only a few people knew anything about: my secondary reality, the world of the unusual, one that was often bizarre and inexplicable.

Early on in my experiences, I began working with a hypnotherapist named Deborah Lindemann. She helped me not only to remember the sometimes hazy details of the abductions but also to cope with my situation in general. She explained that the human mind tends to filter out anything that does not fit into a person's carefully spun worldview. The mind chooses predictability. It likes to attach a shadow to a figure rather than to see the shadow by itself. The mind does not like "high strangeness." Unfortunately, high strangeness was the new norm for me.

While Deborah was an expert hypnotherapist, she didn't quite know how to deal with an unusual phenomenon that arose during my regressions on August 20, 2004. The regression started out as usual, with me reliving my many abduction experiences in great detail—this included experiencing the physical pain and fear of those events. At the end of this particular regression, I was recounting meeting a terrifying creature, a Mantis being.

The Mantis Encounter

The Mantis creature is a being of few words. As far as my experiences go, he was the boss of the Zetas. My encounter with the Mantis scared the hell out of me. It also confused me greatly and still does to this day. I recall being strapped to a table and seeing the Possum Lady as well as one we called Grandpa Grey with this very large bug creature. The Possum Lady then told me that she had to leave, and that I would be all right. Grandpa Grey didn't say anything to me, but he disappeared as soon as she did, leaving me with only the Mantis and the flock of Greys that were rushing around the room.

My recollection is of lying on a table, feeling the pain and watching the horrible things that the Greys were doing to my body, such as removing fluids and other samples. I could hear them communicating the need to be quick (my interpretation) in delivering the samples. So I asked them, "Why are you in such a hurry—why do you have to be quick? What do you have in those little boxes? Where are you taking them? What are you using sperm for?"

Suddenly, as if the Mantis could read my mind, much like I could hear the thoughts of the Greys, he was looming over me, demanding, "How can you hear us?!" At least that is my simple interpretation of a very complex thought or feeling, but it was more *How do you understand us, or (perhaps) perceive of our thoughts?* Even though the creature was more surprised than angry with me, I was still startled and terrified of this giant, intimidating bug. I began to thrash around as if I was trying to get away, then I nervously answered, "I don't know! I don't know!" The Mantis effectively rendered me unable to hear them or recall anything else that happened during that abduction. No matter how hard I tried under regression, he would suddenly be right there in the room with me, not in my memory but there, somehow invisible, telling me I was not allowed to remember and not allowed to talk about it. It got to the point of somehow taking control of my body and mind.

During the last ten minutes of the session, Deborah asked, "Why is the Mantis so angry at you?"

"I don't know. He wants to know how I can understand what they are saying. I tell him that I don't know."

"Can you tell me what happened next, Stan?"

"He won't let me tell you. He won't let me remember."

"It is safe to remember now, Stan. It is safe to tell me what happened. He's not here, Stan. He no longer has control over what you remember; he can't hurt you," Deborah soothed.

"I can't tell you—he won't let me, he won't let me, he won't let me," I repeated. And that's when something strange started to happen. Suddenly my fearful thrashing fell calm. My body movements were very stiff and controlled, and my voice pattern became very methodical. It was as if someone flipped a switch. It seemed that either I was having some kind of mental episode, or a consciousness not of my own (but also not that of the Mantis) was trying to speak through me.

"It is not allowed. I cannot tell you."

Whatever it was frightened Deborah enough that she immediately brought me out of the regression. Coming out of this session, I felt like I'd just woken up from a long nap. While the sessions

I had gone through before left me with complete memory of what had happened, the last ten minutes of this session were a complete blank for me. When I came to, I noticed surprised expressions around the room. It wasn't until after we left that Lisa explained what had happened. At first I didn't believe her. Luckily we tape all the regressions and once I watched the video and saw it for myself, there was no disputing it. And this was only the beginning!

Although I feel highly uncomfortable with the word "channeling" (reminds me of cheesy New Age gurus claiming to get unusual information from other dimensions, information which may simply have come from an outpouring of an alter ego or the deep subconscious mind), I became increasingly curious about what this "other consciousness" might be trying to say through me. It was for this reason that Lisa and I decided it was time to seek help from someone more familiar with abductees.

After an extensive search, we were finally introduced to Ronald Leo Sprinkle, Ph.D., one of the world's most renowned hypno-therapists specializing in regressing UFO abductees. Dr. Sprinkle has extensively researched the phenomenon of alien abductions. He received his doctorate in psychology at the University of Missouri and founded the Rocky Mountain Conference on UFO Investigation.

Dr. Leo Sprinkle, more than anyone else, has helped me remember and integrate the Consensus and Secondary Realities so that I can make sense of my life.

My first regression with Dr. Sprinkle, on September 30, 2006, went a long way in revealing what had happened during my session with Deborah—because it happened again. This time, though, was different; this time he let it happen.

During this and future sessions with Dr. Sprinkle, we would learn that the other consciousness actually had a benevolent nature and was seeking to infuse my life with critical information. It provided information on numerous topics that had baffled me, including startling information about the time-shifting ability of my star children and how the eldest had visited me many times in my life, keeping an eye on my well-being and my mission. Whatever this thing was, it was smarter than anyone in the room. Through my mouth, it was using words and concepts we had never heard before. On several occasions while watching the filmed regressions, I had to look up words in the dictionary to understand their meaning. The voice or consciousness even revealed how the moon was formed.

It also seemed to have the ability to read minds, and on many occasions would answer a question before it was finished being asked. There were times when Dr. Sprinkle would hand me, or should I say "it," a pen and paper then observe as I jotted down advanced physics equations. Moreover, I was able to write them with my eyes closed and my head turned to the side. Witnessing this left little doubt that the information being channeled through me was from an external source.

During one session, Dr. Sprinkle asked the consciousness for its name, and it responded that it could be called Grandpa. According to the voice, we had mistakenly captured it on film. Everyone assumed that it was talking about the encounter that I had in Colorado Springs, where I videotaped a being watching me through our back sliding-glass door.

When asked, however, if they were one in the same, the answer was no.

"By the fence, by the fence," it replied.

In looking back through our library, we realized I had indeed captured this ET in a different picture and the video was of something or someone else. We also learned that the channeled voice was not a Grey, but a True Orion, and that it chose the name Grandpa simply because my subconscious mind found it comforting; it also gave Dr. Sprinkle someone to address as he asked questions.

As the regressions continued, we learned that there's lots of life in our own galaxy, including different species of Greys. Some short, some tall. Some were "good," some were "bad," and some weren't even grey-colored but had similar features. What I found

This picture was taken when we heard noises out by our back deck.
We found nothing out of the ordinary until we later looked at the pictures.

most interesting was the fact that some of them wanted my work to succeed, and some didn't.

We learned that this particular Orion was from a system six light years beyond Alnitak in the Belt of Orion, and that they had a good view of the Horsehead Nebula.

When Dr. Sprinkle asked if they were willing to tell us more about their civilization, Grandpa responded, "It is beyond your understanding in most. We do not bicker, we do not have war. Primitive cultures fight with themselves."

Dr. Sprinkle then asked, "Have you monitored humans for a long time?"

"Yes," Grandpa replied.

"Do you have information about human origins, about how humanity began on Earth?"

"It was not by us."

"More advanced?"

"As advanced as we are from you, they are as advanced and more from us. Humans are a conglomerate; they are part of the planet you call Earth, and they are more." Grandpa seemed at an usual loss for words to articulate human understanding. He continued, "There are offshoots that do not belong with humans but in the struggle to...to find the origins, humans have...accepted that they are from...word...from this particular species. In fact, they are a conglomeration of off-world and on-world...older than they think. They [the offshoots] existed when what you call cave men existed, but in smaller groups, in little pockets.

"In other planetary systems?" Leo asked.

"They [the offshoot beings that lived among the cavemen] were designed to inhabit and survive here. And we did not understand; we did not have any part...they are...we do not know why. We did not have any part in this."

As my session continued, so did the information, and things were starting to come into focus.

"So, your groups are supportive of humans? And there are groups who are not supportive?"

"Yes," Grandpa answered. "Just like there are groups of humans who are supportive and not supportive. Those who use evil for gain, who live by greed, are creating their own chaos. Because humans are still tribal, wars are being falsely waged by those of greed, using lies. You are on the brink of no return. We have chosen to speed up the learning process so there is a chance to correct the damage. And the human race can save itself. Humans are at a crossroads. They are being judged and they are being guided both by those who are evil and those who are good. There are those who do not see the benefit of the human race succeeding. Yet there are those who do, who will argue the point. The dark cabal is losing ground. There is war! There is a war between their factions. There are those who want this information made public and those who don't. There are those who are being enlightened and this is wonderful. We are excited. But there are those who will do anything to stop this information from coming forward. We are closely monitoring this. We believe enlightenment will happen despite them. Those who will not choose enlightenment will perish. But it is our hope that you [as a people] are strong."

Dr. Sprinkle continued his questioning. "Do you speak as one entity or do you speak as many?"

"There are many. We are just a small group. We monitor and we watch, and if possible we guide," Grandpa responded.

As it was with most of my regressions, there were a lot of people attending and all were allowed to ask questions. Finally one of the attendees asked about the children that we were starting to see, explaining that we were concerned and wanted to know that the children were okay.

"They cannot survive with Stan," Grandpa replied. "He knows this. They are well taken care of. What we are learning from Stan and others helps us to care for the offspring. We are trying to learn. That is the process. We are learning, just as Stan and others are learning from us."

Heidi was also there attending the regression, along with all my other friends and supporters. She, too, had a question. "Will we be allowed to meet them, Victoria and I?

"Sometime, yes," Grandpa replied. "It is not what you expect. The children do not think like humans think. Humans need nurturing. At first we were confused. Some have perished because we did not understand. They are not like humans. These will survive. These are accelerated [in their growth]. Human children take years [to develop]. These children surpass that."

Another attendee then asked, "What genetic characteristics do humans have that interest you?"

"You are a sturdy race. You heal fast," Grandpa answered.

The questioning continued with Dr. Sprinkle. "Do you have information about the lady who visited Stan in his childhood? Is that something you can share with us?

"Yes," Grandpa said. "Offspring!"

Everyone's mouth dropped.

"Stan's offspring?" Dr. Sprinkle responded.

"Stan's offspring. She is Stan's offspring."

Dr. Sprinkle was extremely confused. "Then how could she be with Stan when he was a child?" he asked.

Grandpa quickly replied, "Humans do not yet understand. There are many ways to travel. Humans do not understand time."

Everyone was amazed at the responses. They curiously watched as the consciousness that was using my body as a sort of virtual reality ride explored the world around it. Anything within arm's length had been picked up and thoroughly inspected, including my camera that it had found in my pocket. And of course since my eyes were closed throughout the session, all this happened with my eyes closed, as if Grandpa were able to perceive through my eyelids.

The following photos were taken during this regression, the first by an attendee, the other by none other than Grandpa after he

Many people attended the regression, including a film crew. Out of the five photos I received from various people, three of them showed what looks like some sort of dome over me while I was being regressed.

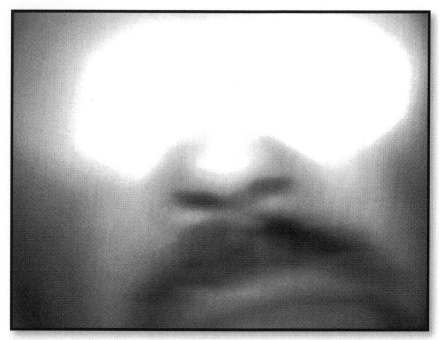

Picture of me that Grandpa took while playing with my camera. I can't explain the white light in place of my eyes.

located our camera in my pocket, snapped the picture, and flung the camera across the room—all the while carrying on a full-blown and detailed conversation with Leo. Is this proof that there is a consciousness working through me?

As impressive as that was, the answers to come in response to Heidi's next series of questions would amaze everyone. "Has Stan seen that woman since he was a boy? Has she been in his life?" she asked.

"Yes," replied Grandpa. "She monitors Stan."

"Do all of his offspring have the ability to—"

As if reading her mind, Grandpa interrupted, "No, she is different. She plays an active role. She is of the Enlightenment. She is highly intelligent."

Dr. Sprinkle then asked, "So she is a hybrid that's able to be here on Earth?"

"Yes, sometimes," Grandpa responded. "She monitors each of you: Lisa, Victoria, Heidi, even you, everybody involved."

After I watched the videotape of the session, I was in a state of mild shock. Although I had learned many things in this regression, what really stood out for me was the story of my hybrid daughter.

I would learn that she goes by the name of Kioma—and that she was the one who visited me as a grown woman when I was a child; who had shown me the tiny globe levitating above her upturned palm; who had accidentally terrified me outside the swimming pool because she could speak without moving her lips; who had made an odd impression on my mother in the parking lot after our Christmas shopping trip. The mysterious woman and the cute little girl were one and the same. When I was a child, my daughter was an adult. And when I became an adult, my daughter came to me as a child. If that weren't mind-boggling enough, I would later learn about her connection to the Audrey calls.

It is one thing to intellectually puzzle over the paradoxes of time-travel, and another to experience its impact on your life firsthand. However, looking back I now realize that if it wasn't for the experiences, I would have never learned what I know or believed that what I was going through was real, let alone possible. It seemed that by confronting what was happening, I was getting pieces of the puzzle one at a time. And now, the information that had been planted in my mind by the Possum Lady was another puzzle that I was about to confront.

Chapter Nine

Predictions

Colorado
May 2008

Jeff Peckman, a prominent personality in local politics, heard my testimony about my encounters and was so moved by my evidence he decided to create something called the Extraterrestrial Affairs Commission for the city of Denver. He hoped that by doing this he would get the public interested in the reality of extraterrestrials. He envisioned a better future for humanity by making the public aware of the benevolent purpose of many ET races. Jeff is working toward the day when people will be open-minded enough to invite the extraterrestrials (ETs) to share their medical technologies, free energy to replace our dependency on petroleum, and advanced space travel technologies with us.

Jeff is interested in ending government secrecy and the flagrant disregard of the law under the guise of "national security" measures, as is our mutual friend Rick Nelson. They both want to end the abuse of the political oligarchy and the Federal Reserve bankers who are depriving Americans of their sovereignty.

By stimulating public interest in other galactic civilizations, they believe the government will be forced to admit that they have known about aliens since the Roswell incident. They are active participants in the rising tide of the Consciousness Movement, whose purpose is to usher in a new era of peace for all mankind, put an end to the massive trauma of wars, and stop the culling of the global population through devitalized foods, GMOs, toxic food additives, chemical trails, mercury-laden vaccinations, and HAARP weather-changing technology.

Although Jeff's campaign was ultimately squashed by political machinations, he accomplished a great deal for the movement. He held a national press conference, where he showed the public my video of "Boo," dubbed "The Alien in the Window" video by the press.

A still from the original "Alien in the Window" or "Boo" video. I thought we had a peeping Tom. Boy was I surprised when I looked at the video!

His actions created a media frenzy. Within hours of the video's release, we were contacted by the folks from the *Larry King Live* show for an appearance. Jeff and I also appeared on CNN. Within a few days, ABC News was knocking on my door.

I invited some crew members from *ABC News 20/20* and *Good Morning America* to my home to learn about my story—nothing was off limits. In fact, I even emptied the contents of my safe deposit box onto my floor. Overwhelmed by all the evidence, Producer Andrea Beaumont was returning materials to their containers when she noticed a manila envelope sitting on a pile of documents. Written on the envelope were the words, "DO NOT OPEN." This took me by surprise because after four years I had completely forgotten about it. In fact, I even forgot why it was in the box in the first place. Only after consulting my timeline journal did I recall the reason the envelope had been sealed and stored away.

I mentioned that the manila envelope might contain predictions. I also admitted that I wasn't sure exactly what was in the envelope.

"We should film it just in case," they responded.

After both producers left, I was torn between exhilaration and self-doubt, agonizing over whether I should even open this time capsule, let alone have them film it. Whatever the contents of this envelope revealed, this could be a turning point—and I knew it.

Not believing in fortune-tellers, I argued with some of my cohorts that opening the package might not be in our best interest. They argued that it would lend my case more credibility. But Rick Nelson reasoned that if the predictions were either not in the package, or inaccurate, it might hurt my case.

I was truly confused about what to do. I had made an informal agreement with ABC, and I didn't want to go back on my word. And what some of my support team suggested made perfect sense: I needed to share the information for everyone's benefit! Unfortunately I still couldn't recall exactly what I had sealed in the envelope, or what I had predicted. I was stumped!

This was when Audrey stepped in. How Audrey knows what is going on as it unfolds still remains a mystery to me.

Andrea, the ABC producer, had accidentally left her cell phone in a pair of pants that she tossed in the washing machine back at her home. When she took the pants out of the washer and discovered the phone, of course she couldn't get it to work. Waterlogged. Then suddenly...it rang.

The Audrey voice said that ABC would not be allowed to film the opening of the predictions. The voice stated that it would endanger everyone involved because the predictions implied that the government was involved in future events that were devastating to the people. Before ending the message, the voice thanked Andrea for assisting me in my quest to bring the truth out to the world. Then the phone died, never to work again.

Bewildered, Andrea called me immediately. She eventually calmed down and said, "I guess we won't be able to film the opening of the predictions after all."

After hanging up the phone, I sat on the couch, amazed. I also heard a clear inner message that warned me I must be careful about disclosing the predictions.

Rick Nelson also received a call from the Audrey voice on his cell phone at exactly the same time as Andrea's call. His message, which he recorded, gave the following instructions:

> Audrey: We apologize. This connection is—how you say—iffy. We are calling to suggest that Starseed open his prediction envelope by next Sunday. Not in front of ABC. If you wait past Sunday, the opposing forces will have time to try to do something.
>
> Rick: I'll make it happen.

While Rick and Andrea were receiving Audrey calls, so was Victoria. She recorded a different message:

> Audrey: Good. You answered. We are already trying to contact Andrea. It has come to our attention that Starseed is allowing ABC to film the opening of the envelope with his—how do you say—predictions. We do not think it is a good idea. We feel that it would be better if Stan were to open it in a more private setting. Some of the contents might be offensive to some organizations, and would only cause disruptions, making things more dangerous to Stan and his family. We will suggest to all involved that this be filmed by someone Stan trusts so that any offending accusations from the predictions may be edited before reaching the public, for Starseed's safety.

All these calls happened simultaneously at exactly 5:50 p.m.

Victoria tried to call me. Since I was on the phone with Andrea, she speed-dialed Lisa. We all decided that Sunday was just as good a time as any to open the predictions.

Since I wanted to open the manila envelope, but not involve the national media, my friends and I decided to open it in private—but to also video record everything in real time and in the presence of reputable witnesses.

Rick Nelson arranged the event at a secure location at our friend Lucie Blanchard's house and invited two Ph.D.s, four established researchers, a deputy sheriff, a venture capitalist, and a few other people close to the project. A videographer, a photographer, and a documentarian were secured to ensure a complete recording of the proceedings. Although Andrea Beaumont was invited, she did not attend, still unsettled by the Audrey call on her electronically inoperable cell phone.

Blanchard residence
Northern Colorado
February 28, 2009

Opening the Time Capsule
With cameras rolling, Rick, Victoria and I tried to describe the "manila envelope and its contents." In the interest of transparency, I confessed that I had forgotten what I had put in the envelope and did not know what to expect.

Almost as nervous as I was, Rick opened the envelope. All eyes were glued on what was inside as Rick pulled out the sheets of paper with my scribbled predictions.

Victoria read the twenty predictions:

Stan Romanek, October 14, 2004, Predictions

1) Early 2005, maybe February or March, military interrupt contact? I think I'm involved maybe?

2) Summer 2005, China floods all over.

3) Early May 2006, I get help? No idea what that means!

4) Late October/early November 2006, UFO tests water for first contact—like a big city, Washington DC, New York or Chicago. Where there will be no doubt! Maybe a military base or airport or large gathering.

5) Mid December 2006, power will go out on millions in the Northwest U.S. They will say it's from bad weather. They will be lying! It will be from UFOs.

6) Summer 2007, government admits 1997 Phoenix Lights are real.

7) Fall 2007 to spring 2008, maybe Mexico, France, or Britain opens UFO files.

8) December 2007, volcano blows in Alaska—ash in all USA.

9) 2008, big time for me. World will know me!

10) Late spring 2008, start of world financial collapse. It's all planned like 9/11.

11) End of June 2008, some UFOs test the waters for first contact again, in England this time.

12) Fall 2008, religion and UFOs (I have no idea!). Another astronaut admits to UFOs.

13) Start of 2009, something big happens. Shift begins—political something. Very big start for me. Also economy very bad! Something about superhighway from north to south.

14) Late spring 2009, winds start because of global warming!

15) Summer 2009, I get help again???

16) US finally admits to UFOs, early 2010, to scare people!

17) 2010, complete world economy collapse, very bad. New World Order takes over. They will fake an attack and nuke New York to create martial law?? (God, I hope not!)

18) 2010, late fall. Something to do with big war? Watch out for Asian countries like China.

19) 2011, Yellowstone erupts! Very, very bad. Then starts first steps to First Contact.

20) 2012, first contact. Everything changes!!!

It was as if Victoria had opened Pandora's Box and unleashed a storm of chaos that could not be put back again. A few attendees, unable to believe what they had heard, asked Victoria to read the predictions again.

Alejandro Rojas, a former chief investigator for MUFON, tapped away on his laptop, checking out the accuracy of global events mentioned from 2005 to 2009.

While Alejandro researched my predictions on the Internet, I filled in the blanks based on my own experiences.

Over the next few hours, we compiled a new list of the verified predictions:

1) Early 2005 maybe February or March, military interrupt contact? I think I'm involved maybe?
   - On January 24, 2005, an orb over my house is caught on tape.
   - On January 25, 2005, 3 UFOs fly over my house in Colorado Springs.
   - On February 2005, I receive a leaked military memo saying they are trying to interrupt UFO visits.
   - On February 6, 2005, my computer is hacked and a CIA logo covers my desktop.
   - On February 19, 2005, my van is fired upon with a High Powered Microwave (HPM) weapon as we are ordering food at a drive through. It instantly fries my engine and electrical system. It takes us hours to get it to a mechanic.
   - On February 23, 2005, I see a lot of black helicopters, as well as military helicopters, hovering over my house.
   - On March 5, 2005, I take a video of Grandpa Grey inside my house.

2) Summer 2005, China floods all over.
   - China floods occurred June 2005. There were 1,024 killed, 293 missing, 900,000 homes ruined, and 10 million hectares (2.4710 acres) of farmland destroyed.[1]

3) Early May 2006, I get help? No idea what that means!
   - On May 6, 2005, my knee is fixed during an abduction, saving me from painful surgery, which may not have been able to correct the injury. On the same day, a scientist figures out the alignment equation date from my planetary drawing is about September 21, 2012.

4) Late October/early November 2006, UFO tests the water for first contact—like a big city, Washington DC, New York or Chicago. Where there will be no doubt! Maybe a military base or airport or large gathering.
   - On November 7, 2006, UFO sightings occur over O'Hare.[2]

5) Mid December 2006, power will go out on millions in the Northwest US. They will say it's from bad weather. They will be lying! It will be from UFOs.
   - There was a storm on December 14th and 15th of 2006. 1.8 million people are in homes without power in the Northwest US.[3]

6) Summer 2007, government admits 1997 Phoenix Lights are real.
   - In March 2007, Fife Symington, the Governor of Arizona, publicly declares that he saw the Phoenix Lights and believed it to be an ET craft.[4]

[1] www.smh.com.au/news/world/china-flood-toll-this-year-reaches-1000/2005/08/31/1125302577104.html

[2] http://en.wikipedia.org/wiki/Chicago_O%27Hare_UFO_sighting_2006

[3] http://en.wikipedia.org/wiki/Hanukkah_Eve_wind_storm_of_2006

[4] http://www.foxnews.com/story/0,2933,260863,00.html

7) Fall 2007 to spring 2008, maybe Mexico, France, or Britain opens UFO files.
   - In March 2007, France discloses UFO government files.[5]
   - In May 2008, Britain opens its UFO government files.[6]
8) December 2007, volcano blows in Alaska—ash in all USA.
   - Although this was the biggest event of the year, it only spewed ash lightly over a few towns.[7]
9) 2008, big time for me, world will know me!
   - On May 30th, Jeff Peckman showed my "Alien in the Window" video to a press conference; then I appear on mainstream television talk shows.[8]
10) Late spring 2008, start of world financial collapse. It's all planned like 9/11.
   - The recession in America and the rest of the world begins appearing in the news.[9]
11) End of June 2008, some UFOs test the waters for first contact again, in England this time.
   - Police helicopters chase a UFO over Cardiff, England.[10]

---

[5] http://www.foxnews.com/story/0,2933,260590,00.html

[6] http://www.foxnews.com/story/0,2933,355509,00.html

[7] http://www.avo.alaska.edu/volcanoes/volcact.php?volcname=Pavlof&eruption id=589

[8] http://www.rockymountainnews.com/news/2008/may/30/alien-commission-causes-commotion/

[9] http://en.wikipedia.org/wiki/Global_financial_crisis_of_2008

[10] http://www.telegraph.co.uk/news/newstopics/howaboutthat/2160814/Police-chase-UFO-over-Cardiff.html; http://www.youtube.com/watch?v=UGgjlB8ZXpQ

12) Fall 2008, religion and UFOs (I have no idea!) Another astronaut admits to UFOs.

- On May 2008, Vatican astronomer says it's OK to believe in UFOs.[11]
- Although Apollo 14 astronaut Edgar Mitchell has been talking about UFOs for years, it makes worldwide headlines in July and August 2008.[12]

13) Start of 2009, something big happens. Shift begins—political something. Very big start for me. Also economy very bad! Something about superhighway from north to south.

- Bush plans on building NAFTA superhighway.[13]
- Barack Obama is inaugurated as the 44th President of the United States on Tuesday, January 20, 2009.[14]

By the time the predictions had been verified, I was so overwhelmed—it took all my effort not to burst into tears.

Rick proceeded to speak directly into the camera: "This almost brought tears to my eyes. It confirms many things. I now understand why we could not open this up on television. Certain authorities would have a problem with it."

If this time line continued the way it was going, the future of mankind looked grim, I thought to myself.

"Why would the ETs give me such information and what am I supposed to do with it?" I asked Rick.

"Your guess is as good as mine," he responded. Maybe they think by giving this to us we can somehow change our own future.

---

[11] http://www.msnbc.msn.com/id/24598508/

[12] http://www.guardian.co.uk/science/2008/jul/26/spaceexploration?gusrc=rss&feed=networkfront

[13] http://www.humanevents.com/article.php?id=15497

[14] http://en.wikipedia.org/wiki/Obama_inaguration

That's just a guess, of course. Other than that, I don't have any answers."

Luckily the answers would come to life sooner than any of us could imagine, and from an unlikely source. What had remained locked in Pandora's Box was released. And a stranger among the gathered group was about to reveal a startling truth.

Chapter Ten

The Resurrection of Hope

People from all walks of life, from scientists to bartenders, had come to watch the opening of the time capsule. I had either invited or been introduced to everyone in the room, except for one elderly gentleman. Turns out, he had quite a lot to say.

Victoria finished her second reading and the room was abuzz with fearful wonderings about the predicted devastation to come. A video camera continued to roll. The elderly stranger's voice calmly rose above the crowd.

"Stan, I must address your comment regarding Pandora's Box. The evil was unleashed into the world a long time ago. And yes, I believe you have opened the box again, but for the betterment of mankind. If you will recall the story, all that remained locked in the 'box' after the evil had been released was hope. You have given hope back to the world. Now is the time for people around the world to be shown that hope is alive, and with it the intended solace—a balm to sooth all fear.

"I have information suggesting a shift had occurred that will change your timeline and the history of the world. With the help of the Angelic Realm and higher-level beings, we have moved into a second timeline that will hopefully move us further away from the possibility of Armageddon, a scenario coming into fruition as a result of the Illuminati creating weather modifications using HAARP technology, scalar weapons, financial Ponzi schemes, and political machinations with oligarchs around the world."

"Who the hell are the Illuminati?" I asked.

"They are a secret organization run by the wealthy elite, and from what I understand they appear to be using the doomsday image of Armageddon as their script. To make matters worse, it seems that they have scheduled 2012 as their year of emergence. At this time, this secret society, which has existed for centuries, will come out of secrecy to rule the world under one totalitarian government. It is rumored that this so-called 'New World Order' will probably obtain obedience through fear and will try to trick the population into injecting a computer chip into their bodies under the guise that it is necessary for safety and well-being. Heck, they might even try to pass it off as some type of immortality device. The chip will be used to track those who resist enslavement. In the Bible, this has been referred to as 'the mark of the beast.'"

"That's outrageous," Rick Nelson said. "Nobody would be dumb enough to allow a government-controlled doctor to inject a computer chip into their body."

I wouldn't be too sure," responded the stranger. "After all, the entire fluoridation scheme worked flawlessly; instead of strengthening enamel, fluoride actually weakens brain functioning. And Monsanto has been very successful in creating GMO foods that increase infertility."

"I guess you're right," muttered Rick. "The mercury-laden swine flu vaccine did very well. If a vial dropped on the floor, they would have to call Hazmat to clean it up, but people were standing in line to get it injected into their body. They were willing to be injected because they feared an epidemic."

I felt that somehow these grim scenarios seemed to fit in with what I had just revealed in my predictions about a complete world economy collapse and the rise of a New World Order after martial law was declared following a fake nuclear attack.

"How do you know all of this?" I asked.

"I have my connections," said the mysterious elderly man. He continued, "You must understand that there is, however, going to be a shift, so there is no need to worry. If what I am being told is true, then your timeline will be off from now on.

"May I be so bold as to ask why you were so upset over the predictions?" he asked me gently.

"I'm scared," I confessed. "While most people just heard Victoria read the predictions, I could see them unfolding in my mind's eye. You have to understand these are implanted memories placed in my mind by the Possum Lady. She didn't talk to me, but sent me thoughts, for lack of a better description. When the thoughts are noble and inspiring, I am calm, but when I envision a horrendous future with natural disaster or war, it brings me to my knees. These thought beams explode in my mind with images, sensations, and feelings. It's like watching a two-hour movie in 20 seconds, and feeling everything as intensely as if I'm immersed in the movie itself."

"As I have said, the timeline has shifted and the Illuminati are losing power. The 'something big that will happen in year 2009' prediction has already begun. Stan, I need you to hear and understand that the rest of your predictions will not come to fruition because of 'the shift.'"

Leaning over to Rick, I whispered, "Who is this guy?"

"Lucie invited him," replied Rick. "He's OK. He spoke at my monthly Paranormal Research Forum meeting a while back."

"Perhaps an introduction is in order," Rick said. "By now everyone is probably wondering who the old wise man is and how he got invited in the first place." Rick waved at Lucie to come forward. "Lucie," he said. "Why don't you introduce Stan to your friend."

"Sure, make me do everything," Lucie replied with a smirk. Lucie glanced over at the mysterious man for approval. Once he nodded his head, Lucie turned around, raised her arm, and said, "Stan meet

John, John meet Stan." Then she shook her head and promptly went back to her chair. Lucie has never been subtle, but she is to the point, and if nothing else she makes all of us laugh.

"Hello, John," I said. "All I know is that whatever this shift is, it's going to be big. Even now it's incredible," I said.

"It's already big," John replied.

"It appears that we are the creators of our futures," said Rick.

Rick is a former Naval Air Intelligence officer. I recall him once telling me how he swam in waters infested with great white sharks. He, more than anyone else in the room, understands what it is like to walk the razor's edge. Being converted from military intelligence to someone who wants the truth exposed about ETs is a hell of a switch and had to be a hard transition.

"That's correct," replied John.

Excited, Rick pitched in, "Indigenous cultures all over the world are talking about this time of cultural transformation. It's the end of the old royal bloodlines that have enslaved mankind for centuries and the beginning of an era of sovereign souls. It will be a time where every man, woman, and child is truly free to express their divine birthright."

Encouraged to share my feelings, I continued. "What people need to understand is that if the remainder of my predictions turn out to be true, it is going to get really bad because billions of the world's population will be wiped out."

"Events are transpiring," Rick droned.

"I want to balance that out," countered John. "All predictions are only probable realities based on what has happened before. The information that comes from the Angelics says that the timeline you were given no longer exists, and that this new shift may bring forth a golden age for humankind; it's what Vedic scholars call the Satya Yuga, the age of truth, a golden age. So, it is quite the opposite of what you're now envisioning. Your predictions are destined to collapse the negative timeline and bring forth a parallel reality, which has until now only existed in an embryonic state of potentiality. While some of your predictions will turn out to be exactly the way you saw them, this will not apply to all of them, thank goodness. Only the less threatening scenarios will happen. In choosing to reveal certain dark truths today about the worst end-game scenarios planned for humanity by the dark cabal, you dissipated their possibility; you collapsed the quantum wave and introduced a new reality. While this alternative reality had already been created by the 'Gathering of One,' it needed a final push to precipitate it. What you are doing, and the opening of your predictions, may well be that decisive thrust, converting possibility into probability. It's bigger than any of you may think," he said, smiling.

"I don't understand how I could collapse an emerging reality," I said. "And what the heck is the 'Gathering of One'?" This John character sounded nuttier and nuttier by the minute, but I continued to listen.

"There is a lot to explain," sighed John. "Do you understand what the butterfly effect is?"

"Yes I do," I replied.

John continued. "By exposing the secret plan for World War III, it seems you are creating a spiritual backlash. When people hear about your predictions, as they will, you will inspire the consciousness movement to create committed meditative practices and spiritual invocations to turn the tide. They will call in the Angelic Realm and the spiritually advanced ET races. You will awaken people, all kinds of people. Spiritual people will send out waves of love and compassion, while earthy, practical people will rally for food cooperatives, community sharing, and peace rallies. You will awaken the sleeping masses from the trance of authoritarianism that has held them in bondage for innumerable centuries."

"Like, they had a war and no one came," I heard someone say in the audience, simplifying his elaborate explanation.

He nodded approvingly. "People only fight wars because they believe the lies perpetuated to incite them. When the lies are exposed, the politicians' inflammatory words fall on deaf ears."

"So, it is as Rick said, we do create our own future." I was beginning to catch the drift of what was happening. "If we don't play along with the darkness and refuse to buy into the mainstream propaganda on television and in the newspapers, we will stop from creating our own destruction."

I suddenly noticed that everything had shifted in the room. People looked at each other with a sense of awe and hope.

"That's absolutely right," said John. "The mainstream media is owned by media moguls who are in cahoots with the dark cabal."

"You asked me about the Gathering of One," John said. "Let me explain. In quantum physics, there is something called a third quantum state. It's the point of choosing. We reached it in September 2008."

"We did?" I asked incredulously.

"In the spring of 2008, I met with a Hopi Elder known as the Keeper of the Secrets and the Prophecies. He revealed a Hopi prophecy not even known to the Hopi people. He said humankind had three chances to bring forth the Fifth World and usher in the Golden Age of Peace."

"Three chances," I echoed.

"In the first chance," he continued, "the Hopi and the Navajo tried and failed. In the second chance, the Utes struggled and faced defeat. Then, the third and last chance was offered to the race least likely to succeed: the White People who had destroyed the indigenous cultures on all the continents of the Earth out of greed for gold or land."

John paused and looked around the room slowly. All eyes were riveted, everyone hanging on to his every word.

Smiling, he resumed his revelation. "During the summer solstice of 2008, I'm told the Angelic Realm asked a group of people to organize The Gathering of One. Over 30,000 people around the world, mostly white, responded to the invitation to visit Yellowstone Park for this event. This event initiated the shift and your revelations today will complete the manifestation of a new earth."

"I don't get it," implored Rick passionately. "Since the time of the Knight Templers, the rich bankers have been accumulating wealth. Today, they control more money than most of the nations of the world. They have all the resources to control governments, as well as the stupendous technology given to them by the supposed negative aliens. How can 30,000 people gathering in one place on earth change everything?"

"Exactly, Rick," said John. "However, now is the time to change all of that. Stan had already gotten that message. He is just not yet aware of what his mission entails. The voice you all call Audrey said, 'Starseed, it's time.' At the same time while we were at Yellowstone, he was being told that now...is the time to..."

"Excuse me, John. I don't mean to interrupt." Suddenly, I understood. The spontaneous knowingness coursed through my body like a divine infusion of pure intuition. "It's not about money or power, nor about monarchies, privileged bloodlines, or military rule. These are examples of force, and like any force in the universe, it has a predictable loss of energy over time. Instead, it's about consciousness, which is infinite power, divine power, the unbridled power to create and dissolve worlds in the blink of an eye. We are all shareholders in this divine power and when a decisive minority votes for change, it precipitates change everywhere. Shift happens when a critical mass in consciousness is reached. It's just like the hundredth monkey thing. Basically we are awakening the sleeping consciousness of humanity by giving the world hope."

"That is exactly right, Stan," John relayed.

"Even now, I try to ignore the messages I get," I replied. "I'm still unsure if it's my mind creating the thoughts or if they are coming from another source. But in light of the already correct predictions that came to me from the Possum Lady, I can't disregard them anymore, especially not now."

Maybe this John guy isn't so crazy after all, I thought to myself.

"They've been running the show through fear," said Rick. "That's why the politicians and the media keep harping on fearful things like wars, terrorists, and street crimes. They want to keep us in a low vibratory state so that we don't remember who we are—spiritual beings having a human experience."

"And the way to get people to listen and to understand it, and to remove the negative control of the elite, is like TV commercials: repeat the truth, reiterate the facts, and reinforce hope until people finally get it," I stated.

"WE are the ones WE have been waiting for," said Lisa. "The people who reverse the fear that has been screwing up our reality. The change makers are actually all of us working together."

Her words touched John. "The elders of the Oraibi Arizona Hopi Nation have spoken of that clearly, Lisa," he said. "I was recently reading about it and liked it so much that I memorized it. Would you like to hear their declaration?"

Everyone was silent, expectant.

Looking into the far distance, John recited the sacred words of the Hopi elders.

"We are the ones we've been waiting for. You have been telling the people that this is the Eleventh Hour. Now you must go back and tell the people that this is The Hour. And there are things to be considered: Where are you living? What are you doing? What are your relationships? Are you in right relation? Where is your water? Know your garden. It is time to speak your Truth. Create your community. Be good to each other. And do not look outside yourself for the leader."

John paused, his voice cracking with emotion. Everyone waited patiently; then, finally, he resumed.

"This could be a good time! There is a river flowing now, very fast. It is so great and swift that there are those who will be afraid. They will try to hold on to the shore. They will feel they are being torn apart, and they will suffer greatly. Know the river has its destination.

The elders say we must let go of the shore, push off into the middle of the river, keep our eyes open, and our heads above the water. See who is in there with you and celebrate. At this time in history, we are to take nothing personally, least of all, ourselves. For the moment that we do, our spiritual growth and journey comes to a halt. The time of the lone wolf is over. Gather yourselves! Banish the word 'struggle' from your attitude and your vocabulary. All that we do now must be done in a sacred manner and in celebration. We are the ones we've been waiting for."

In the silence that fell, I recalled the words of the Audrey voice, captured as an EVP by one of many paranormal teams doing an investigation at our house: "Starseed, it's time."

I finally understood what she had been telling me. It was time for me to wake up. It was time for me to fulfill my mission—to be a messenger—to awaken the world.

Suddenly the silence was shattered by a thunder of conversations. Everyone began talking about all of the information that had come forth in the past hour. I slipped away to the kitchen where John sat alone and silent. "Thank you for the insight you provided, John," I said shaking his hand.

"Stan, I have to confess, when Lucie invited me here today I wasn't sure why. I consulted my guides and they gave me no answer. I'm guided in much the same way you are. Our guides may be different, but I now understand that they are working toward the same goal. At first I thought I was guided here to impart the knowledge that I possess. I'm supposed to teach you something, but it is more than that. I am getting a clear message that I am supposed to help you see who you really are. There is much more to you than meets the eye, and you yourself can't even see it."

"I have a weird feeling that you're right, John. This might sound strange and I'm not sure why this is in my mind but this whole situation has made me think of the raising of Lazarus story from John 11. Have you heard of it?"

"I have," John said with a smile.

"As I said, it might sound strange, but in the story Jesus was called upon by Lazarus's sisters to heal him when he was sick, but Jesus wasn't in a rush to heal him. He had already proven that he could heal the sick and the blind. He had a new lesson to teach. So, when Jesus arrived, Lazarus was already dead, and his sisters were angry and confused. They had put their faith in the Savior and they felt that he had failed them. Jesus had allowed them their anger before he resurrected Lazarus. The resurrection of Lazarus showed not only the sisters but also the people that hope is as strong as faith. That being said, I know I am in no way any kind of savior but I can't help feeling like I am being placed by the ETs in a similar situation, to teach the people, and restore hope," I said, feeling totally overwhelmed.

"Stan, you are right, but you are not the savior. You are Stan—a simple man. And that, my friend, is what makes you so special; that is where your power lies."

"I realize I'm not the savior, John. But at the same time, I want to help everyone," I said.

"You can't save everyone. I know it is in you to want to try, but all you can do is share the information and allow others to choose. That is the point of being here at this time. It is as I've said before: It is the point of choosing."

I simply smiled as calm settled over me. "John," I said, "would you mind if I gave you a nickname?"

"That depends on what it is," John retorted, grinning from ear to ear. "I have been called many things in my life, and some have not been very nice."

"I'll call you Lazarus! That way I won't forget the lesson you taught me today."

"Lazarus...I like it, it's kind of catchy. I will agree to it, on one condition."

"What condition?" I asked, confused.

"Stan, you have to admit to yourself that I didn't teach you this lesson, you came to this understanding on your own. I simply guided you to it."

"It's a deal, Joh—Lazarus," I said.

"Stan, when you are ready to explore who you really are, you contact me. I will help you see what you have forgotten. You have to want to see. I can only guide."

After that exhilarating encounter with the stranger I now referred to as Lazarus, I ironically found myself filled with the most agonizing self-doubt. My thoughts stirred.

Could I have been subject to genetic engineering before I was born, and why?

Why did the mysterious woman come when I was five, eight, and ten to inform me that I was here on the earth to do something special?

Why did strange beings from other planets abduct me and fill me with ideas that would turn out to be true? Mathematical equations that pointed toward the riddle of space travel; galactic maps that showed hidden planets and unrecognized star systems; predictions that would alter the fate of life on Earth for all living beings?

All I wanted to do was unpack my collection of Native American flutes and play a haunting melody by the banks of a winding river beneath the moonlight. As a person with some Cree Indian ancestry, the rhythms of a natural, spontaneous life appealed to me immensely. I did not want to be special. In fact, I craved the fate of an ordinary man and indeed, looking within, all I could see was how much I was like everyone else.

"I know I'm not the savior," I said to Lisa one night as we sat on the deck in the backyard watching the canopy of stars above. "It's just really in my heart to help as many people as I can. That's all I really want to do."

"Stan," she said, "quit whining and get on with your life. You have a job to do and you know it."

"What life? I don't know what I'm supposed to do. I'm supposed to have answers for people and I don't even know who I am."

"You have been chosen, for Christ's sake," she said.

I smiled feebly, "Couldn't they pick on someone else?" I complained. "It's not like I volunteered for the job."

"Perhaps you did," said Lisa. "Maybe on some other level and you just don't remember? Perhaps you chose to be a messenger, one who discovered precious stones in his own backyard and was assigned to deliver them to humanity from his bright red pedal car. And maybe it is time to deliver the answers to the world that they have been seeking for millennium."

"How can I be a messenger?" I protested, "I feel like such an ordinary man...maybe I'm just nuts."

Lisa shook her head and laughed.

"That's why you're the messenger...because you ARE ordinary and a little nuts. Could very well be that the message needs to be delivered by a common nut ball," she said with a grin.

Despite my misery, I had to chuckle. Lisa had a knack for saying just the right thing in the most amusing way to make me laugh.

"Who am I?" I repeated.

"Perhaps it's time to find out, Starseed," she said in a mock British accent. Not even the noble ETs who we thought spoke through the Audrey voice were spared her wit.

"How?" I asked. I knew Lisa well enough to know that she was leading up to something.

"Call Lucie!"

"Lucie?"

"Lucie can put you in touch with that Lazarus guy who stole your show. She brought him in; they must be friends."

"I'm not quite sure about him," I protested. "He seemed awfully strange. He kind of reminded me of a cross between a mad scientist and a swami. In fact, I wonder if he's crazy."

Lisa was looking at me intently as I pondered over the old man who had made such a powerful impact on us. Her wise blue piercing eyes, magnified in intensity by her glasses, looked at me as if she could read my thoughts. Sometimes it scared me to think that she found me so predictable.

"Just call Lucie and get his number," she said. "It might be a complete waste of time—or, he might just know how to help."

Instead of calling Lucie, I used the excuse that I needed a little break to relax and rest before ABC returned and filming of the 20/20 program began. I have to admit I was scared. My last encounter with Lazarus, the crazy old guy, had filled me with a lot of questions, and I was a bit freaked out to learn what answers might be revealed.

Chapter Eleven

Discovering My Mission

March 2009
Northern Colorado

"Do you think Lazarus will meet with me?" I asked Lucie.

"Well, I could ask him."

Years ago, Lisa and I met Lucie at a seminar. As our paths continued to cross, we became dearest of friends.

"He has an unlisted number," said Lucie. "So I'll have to call him for you."

"That's fine," I said.

By this time, Lisa was also working on a book, *From My Side of the Bed: Pulling Back the Covers on Extraterrestrial Contact—A Spouse's Point of View*, and had met her editor through Lucie, barely a week after we read off the predictions. It was Lisa's new editor who suggested that Lisa was in a struggle to "find her own story" or something along those lines. He was disappointed that Lisa's book was not her story, but was in fact *her* version of *my* abduction story. He then elicited the assistance of another person Lucie also knew, to help Lisa understand how important she was. And how important her role in my life—my experience—was.

Lisa had just returned from her meeting with "the wily old coot," as she called him. "Really, Stan, you have to meet this guy," she urged. "I think he could really help you, too. He's very smart, but it's like he can see inside your mind. It's kind of freaky how he just knows stuff."

"I'm sure he is a nice guy," I said. "But I have enough freaky crap to deal with. I need answers, not more questions." I had plans of my own, and Lisa's new friend was of no interest to me. I knew I was supposed to meet with Lazarus. Somehow I knew he could help me find answers.

Shortly after the conversation with Lisa, Lucie walked out of the room and returned a few minutes later, handing me the phone.

"It's Lazarus," she said, winking.

I could hear laughter coming from the phone. Apparently, he really liked the nickname I had picked out for him. We quickly arranged an appointment: In two weeks, Lisa and I were to meet Lazarus at Lucie's house.

Lucie's house
2 weeks later

Lisa had been acting strangely for the past couple of days—since her last meeting with her "woo-wooey wily old coot" friend. It was as if she had a secret she was trying desperately to hide, and yet she was so excited about something that she could barely hold it in.

As we entered the house, I saw Lazarus sitting at the dining room table, his cane leaning against the wall. It appeared that he was drinking tea and talking to someone on the phone.

Not wanting to disturb him, Lisa and I both took off our shoes to walk quietly. Just then I overheard Lazarus say something about having worked at the "puzzle palace." Thinking it had to do with a retail game store or something, I blew it off.

Once he noticed that we were there, he said his goodbyes to the person on the phone and then turned to greet us.

"Hello, Stan. You don't look good," he said kindly. "I hope it's not catchy. Hello, Lisa," he said, hugging my wife and kissing her cheek.

"Hello, John," Lisa replied, grinning from ear to ear like the little imp that she is. I couldn't figure out what she was so giddy about. That's when she turned to me, "Honey, this is my friend, John. You know, the 'wily old coot' I've been trying...to tell you about," she said as she burst out laughing.

I sat down at the table, stunned. I hadn't bothered to find out who this "wily old coot" person was that was helping Lisa. Lucie, too, had obviously found great pleasure in watching me reject assistance from Lisa's new friend, demanding that only Lazarus could help me, when in fact we were talking about the same person the entire time.

"So, why do you look so sickly today?" repeated Lazarus.

"I've been chronically ill," I confessed. "And my doctors can't seem to figure out what it is. It began in 2007 when I started having some neurological problems. I was misdiagnosed with tetanus."

"It's more than ill health, isn't it?" he asked.

"Yes...I'm having some kind of existential crisis. I feel I've been given unique experiences and access to privileged knowledge to help humanity, but I don't really want to be a messenger."

"I understand, you just want to have a normal life," he acknowledged. "You want to work a regular job and raise your family. You want to go on fishing trips in the summer. In fact, it really isn't that much fun being a bestselling author and giving interviews on radio shows. You want an ordinary life, full of the simple pleasures of ordinary living. Tapping the deep information welling up from your own subconscious mind disturbs you. But, my friend, staying ordinary will not make life easier."

"That's it exactly," I said.

"It's embarrassing how he can read people," said Lucie, sympathetically.

"It's a gift," he chuckled. "Let's just say that I sometimes have waves of intuition."

"I do too," I said. "I know what it feels like. I have a name for my bursts of intuition: spontaneous knowingness."

Lazarus sipped his tea and nodded slightly, silently encouraging me to say more.

"It's such a relief to hear that someone else has experienced what I'm experiencing," I said. "I would suddenly know things and start to understand entirely novel concepts. For the longest time I kept this to myself because it was bad enough I had to deal with all this UFO and ET stuff. I had no clue how in the hell to explain my hunches! So, I'm more than a little relieved to find out that I'm not the only one."

"But there's more..." hinted Lazarus.

"He's good!" I said to Lucie. She chuckled, enjoying my shock.

"I just get this sense that there is something more," said Lazarus. "I don't know what it is, but I have an intuition that it's something you need help understanding."

"Only a few people know about it," I said. "Understand I feel weird talking about this. Apparently, I have the ability to heal. It started a few years ago when a longtime friend of my wife would come over to visit. Every time I got close to her, my back would hurt. As an experiment, I asked Lisa's friend if her back hurt. 'Oh my God, yes!' she said. 'How did you know? I have fibromyalgia and I'm in constant pain.' It was apparent that what I was feeling was a manifestation of her pain accruing in my body. In other words I could feel her pain. Following my intuition, I reached around to rub her back. Instinctively using my feelings to guide my hand, I went right to the spot that hurt her most. 'Really, how the hell did you know?' she wanted to know. 'I have no idea. It just happened,' I told her. Suddenly my hands started to heat up as if on fire, and after rubbing her back for a while, I was as amazed as anyone to discover that her pain had vanished."

"Why do you keep it secret?" asked Lazarus.

"I didn't understand how I could heal others spontaneously. It unnerved me," I said. "From that point on, things were different for me."

The old man's eyes were soft with compassion. He looked at me as if he could read my mind. "Stan," he said warmly, "you're not an ordinary man, no matter how hard you pretend to have no power in the world. Things are not happening to you, they are happening *through* you. There is a message that needs to be delivered and you are the reluctant messenger."

"I just feel terrible all the time," I complained. "I'm sick more days than I'm well and I'm confused more times than I'm clear-headed."

"If it's any comfort," Lazarus said, "these feelings are only due to your identification with 'ancient mind.' Mind is not personal, although we personalize it. Your thoughts are not your thoughts, but drawn from the gulf stream of all human suffering through the ages."

"Let's start there," I said. "You appear to have some idea about what I'm here to do. When I was little, a mysterious woman told me that I was to do something important when I grew up. Well, I still don't know what that might be."

"I don't know, either," said Lazarus, "but I suspect you have a special mission. I believe I can help you find the answers that you seek."

"How?" I asked, wondering if this guy was for real.

"Come closer. I'll show you."

Using a chair and his cane as a brace, Lazarus stood up. Closing his eyes, he appeared to meditate for a few minutes.

"Take off your jacket," he said. "I want to read your energy field more clearly."

Great, I thought to myself. *This guy is a nut job for sure*.

"You obviously got your jacket from a thrift store...it has someone else's miserable etheric energy cloaking your own field," he announced without missing a beat.

I took off my jacket and tossed it on the back of a chair, slightly embarrassed that he had discerned my frugal buying habits.

"Your body's out of balance. You're dehydrated and low on electrolytes. Your adrenals are taxed and your heartbeat is too rapid because of your self-imposed stress. Part, but not all, of your illness is a direct result of your chronic worry."

"How do you know these things?" I asked.

"Will you just be quiet and listen," said Lucie. "He's trying to help you."

I turned to Lucie and jokingly stuck my tongue out at her. My interruption appeared to distract Lazarus and a long silence followed as he refocused. Perhaps it was intuition. Perhaps he could read my aura. Perhaps he was channeling from the Angelic Realm. Or perhaps my interpretations didn't really matter.

He began speaking in a low voice, as if translating some inner dictation into language.

"Stand in front of me about five paces away. Step forward three paces. Raise your right arm and resist while I press on it."

He pushed on my wrist, and although he was a frail old man, I could not keep my arm up.

"Now take three steps back," he ordered.

What do I have to lose? I thought.

I did as he instructed and he began to pick at some invisible threads in the air. He looked as if he were working on a loom. I began to feel a sense of expansion, imagining that my energy field was plumping up like helium filling a balloon.

He asked me to step forward and did the muscle test once again. My arm was as firm as an iron bar.

"Can you tell the difference?" he asked.

"What did you do?" I asked, amazed.

"Your polarity was reversed because of your stress."

He tapped my sternum and then began to hobble around me. Like some fanatical medicine man, he began to clap his hands and was mumbling something under his breath.

Then he stood in front of me, smiling broadly.

"What did you say?" I asked.

He chortled like the crazy old man I thought he was.

"Oh, all I said was, 'Above and above, below and below, above and below.' Then I said, 'Right and right, left and left, right and left.' Finally, I said, 'As above, so below, as below, so above; as right, so left; as left, so right.'"

"Why?"

"I was just fine-tuning your etheric filaments. They are like strings on a guitar and I was plucking on them to recondition them. Eastern mystics call them the *nadis* of the subtle body."

"Weird," I muttered.

"You don't know the half of it," commented Lucie, grinning.

Lisa laughed. I glanced at her. She was sitting in the far corner of the room, watching me, amused at the expression on my face and my obvious attempt to understand what was going on.

Yet despite the strange treatment, I did feel better, as if I had just woken up from a deep and restful nap. Lazarus then began a range of strength tests on me, mumbling inaudible questions. My extended arm remained strong and true.

"Just shifting quantum reality, tweaking it here and there," he said mysteriously.

"I don't understand," I said, laughing nervously.

"It doesn't matter," he said. "Your body is doing the re-learning."

I was feeling remarkably clear-headed by this time and curiously happy for no reason at all.

"Your color has returned," Lucie volunteered. "You look like a newborn right after the doctor slapped your ass. However, I do think he may have held you upside-down a little too long."

This was Lucie's typical Louisiana humor. Everyone laughed.

Exhausted, Lazarus had to sit down. His fragile arm trembled from the strain of holding his cane for so long.

"Damn, I'm getting old," he said, apologetically.

I pulled my jacket off the chair, preparing to leave. Lazarus looked at me with alarm.

"Wait, we're not done," he said. "I want to put you in an angelic gateway. We can do it here in the dining room."

I looked around nervously at Lisa. She nodded, encouraging me to stay the course. Knowing Lisa as well as I did, I guessed that she was amused by all of this and curious about what could happen.

"It's not as frightening as it sounds," said Lazarus, whose kindly nature had a calming effect on me.

He then grabbed a chair from the table and placed it in the middle of the floor. Walking around it, he spread semi-precious stones on the floor in a diamond-shaped pattern. He appeared to be sorting out the stones from his basket and arranging them by color groups. Once he had arranged everything perfectly, Lazarus motioned toward the chair.

"Come, take a seat," he said.

Reluctantly, I stepped carefully around his stone pattern and sat down in the chair.

He asked me to close my eyes and begin breathing slowly, inhaling through my nose and then exhaling through my mouth. Soon, I was breathing deeply and rhythmically.

Oh my god, I thought. What am I getting myself into? This guy is whack-a-doodle.

As I listened to Lazarus's voice, my breathing began to deepen, lulling me into a state of even deeper relaxation.

He instructed me to focus on a world of my own creation, based on safety and peace. It wasn't a guided meditation, but more like a managed introspection. The technique, explained Lazarus, allowed quantum realities to come forward. Having no idea what he was doing, I allowed myself to be open-minded and curious.

As my breath deepened, it was as if each breath was improving the vision of my mind's eye. It got to the point where I could see so vividly that I wondered if I might be hallucinating.

The colors throughout my surroundings suddenly intensified and became so vivid I was startled and gasped in surprise. Light surrounded me as if reflected from the rocks. Pictures formed in front of me, and I felt like I was immersed in a movie.

My eyes opened. Although I was tempted to freak out, I allowed myself to remain curious. Fields of colored energy surrounded everyone in the room. As the energy increased, the walls appeared to turn translucent. The Czech side of me was ready to jump out of the chair while the Cree side of me felt like I'd come home. The familiarity of the feelings and the change in my surroundings made me feel that I had returned to the real world. It almost seemed as if ordinary reality was an imaginary, false world.

Lazarus was quiet, perhaps sensing what was about to happen.

My mind's eye became the true eye overshadowing what my physical eyes would normally see. I realized I had a choice of which world to dwell in, which one to see.

Normally, I would run in panic from such an experience. But the sheer comfort of it, the undeniable familiarity of it, completely drew me in.

Off to my left, a being walked in, appearing to have entered through an invisible door. It was completely bathed in multi-colored light.

As each minute passed, the alternate world intensified to the point where the notion of fear became impossible, a joke.

I carefully listened to the rainbow-colored being addressing me. As he spoke, he transmitted a unique energy and my fingers and toes tingled.

"Where is this coming from?" I asked myself. "What's happening to me?"

Like a slow wave washing through me, the tingling grew, taking over my whole body. The electric colors around the rainbow, as vivid as a Van Gogh painting, took my breath away!

The multicolored being tossed a series of scenes before me like a shaman.

This Rainbow Spirit hinted that I was from somewhere else, somewhere far from the Earth. He said that my home world was close to Orion, and that I came from a world populated by priests. Their culture, their system of governing, was completely based on spiritual principles. They considered all life holy, all beings sacred, and every world blessed. Listening to the sheer beauty of their perspective made me feel light-headed. My senses felt elevated, giving me the ability to connect to everyone in the room, heart to heart, mind to mind, and essence to essence. I could not stop what was happening to me, nor did I want to.

I turned to Lisa. I wanted her to share my experiences, to feel the magnificence of what was about to embrace our Earth. Tears welled up as I saw the link between all of humanity and the priestly people.

As I continued to stare at Lisa, I felt compelled to tell her, "I see you fully. Your struggles show up as if they are clothing. You don't have to wear this clothing. You don't have to worry so badly. Everything is going to be fine. We simply have to allow it to come forward."

I looked over at Lucie. Knowing that I was reading the fields around her, she pointed a finger at me. "Hey, don't even go there," she ordered. "You know too much already. Just keep it to yourself. If I wanted a reading, I'd hire a gypsy."

Everyone laughed, defusing the gravity of the unfolding phenomena.

I would have laughed too but the power of the Rainbow Spirit grew even stronger. I tried to look into its eyes, but its face was so brilliant I could see no features. It stood a good ten feet in height, towering above Lucie's dining room. Its energy reached past the vaulted ceiling as it worked through me.

"Oh my God," I said, now looking at Lazarus. "I understand."

All of a sudden, it was if a grand plot had been revealed. Knowing what was coming frightened me—not because it was negative, but because I began to question whether I deserved to be a part of it, whether I was worthy of playing a heroic role in a divine play where I felt like a buffoon.

"Who can possibly believe what I'm seeing?" I asked aloud.

"It's OK," comforted Lazarus. "Just tell me what you see."

As I began to tell him what had unfolded in front of me, I realized that saying it made it more real. Moreover, hearing myself speak made it more tangible. Unexpectedly, tears gushed like rain water down my cheeks.

After I finished divulging what I knew, Lazarus said, "I am here to tell you that everything you said is true. But I must also tell you that if you will learn to own your power, if you will give up your victimhood, nothing will be able to stop you from giving this world information that will allow every man, woman, and child to co-create a New Eden and open a gateway to complete transformation."

Then, in my mind's eye, I caught a glimpse of the future:

Wealth would be unlimited because we would no longer see ourselves as slaves of debt but as a creative culture.

War would come to an end because our vision of creative possibilities would expose war as nothing more than absurd waste of life.

Overpopulation would no longer be a threat to our existence as we explored new worlds far beyond our own—like the time our forefathers first discovered America and considered it a Brave New World.

This vision made me take a closer look at myself. *How could I believe what just happened?*

Telling people what I was seeing would make me look like a weirdo. "I can't go on anymore," I said, standing up and stepping outside the stone geometry. The astounding energy folded in on itself and evaporated.

"I can't go on," I repeated. "I really hate New Age crap. And I'm starting to sound like the people I can't stand. This isn't me. I can't do this."

Lazarus smiled in a knowing way. "I have to tell you, Stan, that you can't unring the bell. Whether you like it or not, you have chosen a path that few can walk. Your Cree ancestors called it the

Red Path. They knew few could tread its ways and they regarded those who dared to carry this burden to be very enlightened and honored them with great respect."

Lucie came to life like an avenging angel. "Yeah, Stan," she shouted. "Get off your lazy ass and kick some butt!"

"Lucie," I said with a grin, "bite me. But take out your false teeth first."

"Where and how hard, Big Fella!"

***

A few days later, as I sat deep in thought about what I had experienced in the gem-laden gateway, Lazarus called me. *How does he do that?* I wondered. *He has a strange ability to know when I'm dwelling on something that I can't figure out.*

"Stan, I believe the time has come to pull back the curtain hiding the Wizard of Oz. Meet me in forty minutes at the Wonderful Dragon restaurant." Without waiting for a reply, he simply hung up.

I chuckled. Laz is the only one I would allow to get away with that kind of behavior. I knew he wasn't being rude; it was simply a matter of urgency in his mind. I also knew that he wanted to help me to better understand my role of messenger and discover my importance. According to him, I had a role to play in creating a new timeline.

Mystified by his rambling description, curious about what he had meant by "timelines," and intrigued by the possibility of finding an answer to my questions about the big picture, I hopped in the van and drove to the restaurant to meet him, still unsure whether he was crazy, or a mystic, or both.

Chapter Twelve

Splitting Timelines

As arranged, I drove the forty-some-odd miles to meet with Lazarus at the Wonderful Dragon. He had arrived a few minutes earlier and was waiting for me in a booth. Waving his arm as soon as I walked in, he greeted me with a handshake and smile.

After I sat down, a beautiful and familiar petite Chinese woman approached us.

"Hi, Stan. How are you? It's been a long time since you've been in to see me. How is the family? Is everything OK for you right now?"

I addressed her as I stood up. "Hi. Ping. I'm doing well," I said, giving her my customary hug. "Ping, this is my friend Lazarus. Laz, this is Ping. She's the owner."

She enjoyed personally serving her favorite patrons. "What can I get you for lunch, gentlemen?" she asked, and after taking our orders she disappeared into the kitchen.

We made small talk about the weather, the fluctuations in the economy, and the Denver Broncos until Ping returned. After quickly placing drinks on the table, she again disappeared into the kitchen. I anticipated that it would not be long before Lazarus got down to business.

After sipping on his cup of hot tea, Lazarus looked at me for a long time as if weighing something in his mind. Then, appearing to come to a decision, he spoke.

"Stan, I've invited you to lunch today because I know how concerned you are about the time capsule predictions. I think it's time to give you the whole story around that. However, you must understand that what I'm about to tell you is going to test you. I believe the reason for your being given the timeline predictions by the Possum Lady was to allow this very story to come forward. Several of the predictions in your timeline have also shown up in statements made by various whistleblowers."

I had never seen Lazarus look so serious. Discomfort crawled through me as I immediately began to wonder why he was telling me this now. Why not sooner?

"I've obtained the information I'm about to share with you over many years. After piecing things together, I realized that what I had stumbled on was so grand that it affects all life on Earth. It's based on my own research and my investigation."

As if to validate his years of research, he pulled out of his briefcase a huge stack of notes and set it on the table. "I'm not sure where to start," he confessed.

"Begin at the beginning," I suggested.

"I'm sure you've heard all kinds of stories about the Roswell crash in July of 1947. What you may not know is that when the craft crashed, it had far more impact than just hitting the ground. The dead bodies that were found were not aliens. They were humans, who didn't look human, and they had traveled back in time."

"Humans? I thought that they were Greys?"

"Not quite. Our human physiology and intellectual capacity had changed—and we had become a type of Grey. But understand, there are different types of Greys."

He paused to let this sink in.

"How did they know they were from the future? And why were they here?" I asked.

"There were technologies that were found, and later back-engineered, that allowed visuals into both the past and the future. However, let me get into that later. The reason these humans had come back in time to 1947 was to help our planet, perhaps even save our planet, from a solar event that was soon to come. That solar event causes so much destruction that it alters Earth's history in a very negative way. So these beings came for very benevolent reasons. Unfortunately, they had miscalculated the state of our primitive technology, so when our military radar disrupted their craft's navigational system, it crashed. On board the craft, the military found a unique technology that they called a black box because they didn't understand its purpose."

"I'm familiar with the idea of a black box," I interjected. "It's used in aviation to provide information about a plane crash. It's actually a misnomer, since it's a bright orange box. The color makes it easy to find in the wreckage. The black box is an audio recording device found in the cockpit of an airplane or a helicopter that records the dialogue between the pilots. It's something immensely useful for investigators trying to determine the cause of the crash."

"That's true enough," said Lazarus, "but this black box was much more sophisticated, involving far more than sealed audio-recording equipment. After some of the best mathematical minds had decoded the information in the black box, it led to the formation of a top-secret program called Project Yellow Book."

"ET phone home?" I quipped.

He was not amused. "The name comes from a time-travel machine on-board craft that emits a yellow light. The light helped them decide how to navigate into the past or the future."

"They found what they thought was a portable time-travel machine?"

"Originally, Project Yellow Book was in the hands of the Air Force. There are rumors that once they realized its sophistication, it was transferred to the National Security Agency, the NSA."

"How in the world do you know all this?" I asked.

"Let's just say I have connections," he replied. Then he paused to take a sip of his green tea.

I knew there was more to Lazarus than he would ever let out, a lot more. There were times I wondered if he was even human. The things he knew combined with his metaphysical capabilities always left me in awe. Then I remembered overhearing his phone conversation at Lucie's house a week or so earlier. *Puzzle Palace?* I thought to myself. *What the heck is the Puzzle Palace?*

Lazarus continued. "This was just the beginning of what they were to learn about time-travel devices. NSA was to later discover something even more remarkable, which they called Project Looking Glass. These devices started out allowing us to see either the future or the past, but later grew into more advanced technology where we were actually able to *travel* to the future or the past. And, as soon as the Looking Glasses became operational, the entire space-time continuum shifted. It seems that what these benevolent beings had inadvertently caused was the emerging of a far worse future than the one they had hoped to prevent—because of our reverse-engineering in creating the Looking Glasses. When the Looking Glasses became operational, they caused a whole new future that then allowed yet even more races from the future to manifest and arrive on our doorstep."

"If time travel is possible," I responded, "it's only because of a change in our perspective of time. Since time occurs simultaneously, it's only our perception that breaks it into past, present, and future. Thus, no real paradox exists in a universal sense. Everything happens at the same time, but only the presence of an observer makes it appear to flow sequentially."

"Yes, that's right," responded Lazarus. "Consider time-travel apparatus as a way to overcome the limitations imposed by localized consciousness. The Looking Glass Project, for instance, was made to be a portal entry mechanism in order to bend space-time. Events over the forward and rear event horizons could be observed."

"Observed, but not heard?" I remarked.

"Yes, silent—until it was paired with another device," he replied.

"So then, the observer could see and hear unfolding events?" I added.

I stared at my own food, too preoccupied to eat. My mind was focused on trying to envision this unusual device. He looked at me intently, as if anticipating more questions.

"Could this Looking Glass Technology be used to do more than observe? Could it be used to travel and communicate?" I continued.

"Attempts were made to find out. Protocols were tried out for two years, specifically from 2003 to 2004, but I'm not sure if they were ever successful. In any case, it seems that what is happening to you is part of the undoing of the mess that has been created."

"I'm really having a hard time believing any of this," I said. "What do you mean, 'I'm part of the undoing'?"

"Like it or not, you and your experiences are involved somehow," Lazarus told me.

It was almost too much to wrap my head around. In the grand scheme of the universe I was, for all intents and purposes, a nobody and yet here I was having a conversation with someone I would have never guessed was real, talking about stuff I never in my wildest dreams could've imagined!

"So, what does this looking glass thing look like?" I asked.

Lazarus spoke slowly, with a faraway look in his eyes, as if seeing it in his mind's eye. "The Looking Glass Project was related to the ideas theorized by Einstein, Rosen, and Podolsky. It was a gigantic device made up of a spherical spinning arc in a rectangular frame constructed of nickel, cadmium, and barium. Underneath it, there was a super-cooled spinning disk. Argon gas was infused into the spinning disk before gravity repulsion matter was injected into the argon gas. They also used heavy materials for the gravity repulsion matter, and a new element obtained from the extraterrestrials called Element 115."

"You know," I said, "I remember writing an equation for that in 2002 during my first regression.

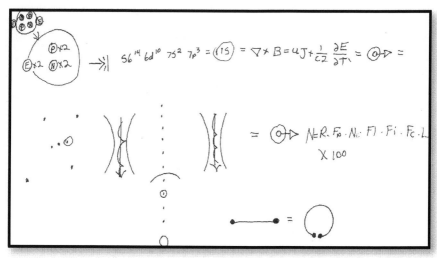

A photocopy of what I drew during my first regression.

"It took the physicists a long time to figure out what it was. Then they said a scientist invented it two years later in 2004." [See photo on following page]

"Yes, I remember," Lazarus nodded. And then he continued, "If you want to see what the Looking Glass looks like, go watch that 1997 sci-fi movie *Contact*. The one adopted from the novel by Carl Sagan and his wife Ann Druyan. People have come forward to say it looks a lot like that machine in the movie."

Images of the movie flashed in my mind:

Jodie Foster played the protagonist, Dr. Eleanor Arroway. Ellie was a SETI scientist obsessed with finding evidence of extraterrestrials at the Arecibo Observatory in Puerto Rico. After scientists discovered secret messages left behind by aliens, they were able to create a huge multi-dimension travel machine contraption. Working together, the nations of the world funded its construction at

6A ★   THE DENVER POST   Sunday, February

Scientists create two new chemical elemen

By James Glanz
The New York Times

A team of Russian and American scientists is reporting today that it has created two new chemical elements, called superheavies because of their enormous atomic mass. The discoveries fill a gap at the furthest edge of the periodic

Scientists create two new chemical elemen

By James Glanz
The New York Times

A team of Russian and American scientists is reporting today that it has created two new chemical elements, called superheavies because of their enormous atomic mass. The discoveries fill a gap at the furthest edge of the periodic table and hint strongly at a weird landscape of undiscovered elements beyond.

The team, made up of scientists from Lawrence Livermore National Laboratory in California and the Joint Institute for Nuclear Research in Dubna, Russia, is disclosing its findings in a paper being published today in Physical Review C, a leading chemistry journal. The paper was reviewed by scientific peers outside the research group before publication.

"Two new elements have been produced," said Walt Loveland, a nuclear chemist at Oregon State University who is familiar with the research. "It's just incredibly exciting. It seems to open up the possibility of synthesizing more elements beyond this."

The periodic table is the oddly shaped checkerboard — with an H for hydrogen, the lightest element, in the upper-left-hand corner — that hangs in chemistry classrooms the world over. Each element has a different number of protons, particles with a positive electrical charge, in the dense central kernel called the nucleus.

The experiments took place at a cyclotron, a circular particle accelerator, in Dubna, where the scientists fired a rare isotope of calcium at americium, an element used in applications as varied as nuclear weapons research and household smoke detectors. Four times during a month of 24-hour-a-day bombardment in July and August, scientists on the experiment said, a calcium nucleus fused with an americium nucleus and created a new element.

Each calcium nucleus contains 20 protons; americium contains 95. Since the number of protons determines where an element goes in the periodic table, simple addition shows the new element to bear the atomic number 115, which had never been seen before. Within a fraction of a second, the four atoms of Element 115 decayed radioactively to an element with 113 protons. That element had never been seen, either.

Joshua B. Patin, a 28-year-old nuclear chemist who is the lead American author on the paper, said he had found it deeply moving to add two more entries to a scientific icon that dates to the 1860s.

That was when the Russian chemist Dmitri Ivanovich Mendeleyev noted clear patterns in the chemical properties of the known elements and arranged them into the periodic table, leaving gaps for other elements that he correctly predicted would some day turn up.

"This is a working piece of art," Patin said. "We're not done yet. Nothing's been finished. What i could really mean down the road nobody can tell. And that's th part that's exciting to me."

Someone sent me this article two years after my first regression, during which I made my drawing. This proves that it was not until two years later that science had the element that I drew.

Cape Canaveral on top of Launch Complex 39. Unfortunately, the machine was destroyed by a religious fanatic, killing David Drumlin, a government scientist who had been chosen to pilot it. However, Ellie was chosen to pilot a second machine that had been secretly built in Hokkaido, Japan. Although she time-traveled, meeting an alien who manifested as her deceased father in a surreal reality, a controversy breaks out because of the substantial time difference between her account of the event and what the cameras caught on tape. She spoke about eighteen hours of experience, but everyone outside the machine perceived that only a few seconds had passed.

"There seems to be a lot of correlations between what's real and what's in the movies," I said.

Lazarus looked up at me. "There is a scene in the movie where Ellie's main critic admits that he cannot explain the eighteen hours of recorded static noise on Ellie's headset, which validates the quantum theory that time could be bent to accommodate both realities," he said. "So the purpose of the movie was more than mere entertainment. The purpose of the movie was to tell the truth, but pretend it was fiction."

"So it was 'hidden in plain sight,'" I commented.

"Although Carl Sagan denied ever finding proof of extraterrestrial life," said Lazarus, "it's remarkable how his machine was a close replica of real extraterrestrial technology. The Illuminati, who own the studios in Hollywood, like to disclose what is real and pretend that it's fictional. The gigantic machine you saw in the movie accurately showed Looking Glass Technology!" [See following page]

"I remember the machine," I said. "There were at least two rings of electromagnets used and the rest of the device was made of a barrel, and the argon gas injected into the barrel. These were the basic components. The magnets spun in different directions and created a charge before the gas was injected into the barrel. Depending on the direction of the spin, time-space could be warped forward or backward by long or short distances in relation to the present. The scientists had completed a map of the exact positions and speeds of the magnets required to reach targeted times both forward and backward. Apparently, images of events at different places, relative to the machine's location, could be picked up and reflected off the gas. Ultimately the machine worked like a total immersion experience."

This is a rendition of the device used in the 1997 movie Contact. It is supposed to resemble the Looking Glass technology.

Lazarus nodded, "You understand things that escape most people."

He has no idea, I thought to myself. Since the start of my experiences I had learned exponentially. I was able to understand concepts that I would not have normally even considered. It was as if I had woken up and I suddenly knew things; I was not sure how.

After nibbling on his sweet and sour pork, Lazarus continued: "You have to account for Hollywood adding its own flourishes. The machine allowed a glimpse into a *multiverse* rather than a universe. In the future-view mode, for instance, you only saw probable realities. While the past is preset, the future can change with new circumstances. Unfortunately, what the movie did not tell us was the potential chaos the Looking Glass Technology introduced into time-space."

"What do you mean?"

"I mean the movie left out the convergent timeline paradox."

Slurping the last of his green tea, he leaned forward to explain: "It soon became apparent that the Greys housed in Area 51, in a section called S-4 deep underground, were not that different from us."

I knew of Area 51 from watching TV, but I never remember hearing where it was located. "Where is Area 51 exactly?"

"Area 51 is within Nellis Air Force Base in Nevada."

I remembered hearing that Area 51 was a secret military base involved with developing experimental top-secret aircraft, along with other things, but I was hoping to use this part of the conversation to try to root out a few more answers on what Lazarus really knew.

"So what happened there?" I asked.

"First of all, you need to understand there is a lot of life out there. Some look human; some do not," Lazarus said. "Some are human, some are not, and some of them are visiting the planet and have been involved with the human species for a very long time."

"This sounds complicated," I replied.

"You have no idea," said Lazarus as he peered into his empty glass. He continued. "It's all about power, and what starts this shift in global power is another crash that occurs in 1953 near Kingman, Arizona. A live Grey is captured along with the craft. This is the first sign of the terrible consequences coming about because of the earlier crash at Roswell. A special group of scientists called Aquarius-J-Rod Team 6 were given the task of communicating with them and taking tissue samples from live aliens. They wanted to find out the cause of the incapacitating medical condition that affected the being's nerves. They worked in an area of S-4 known as the Clean

Sphere, a special environment designed to meet their atmospheric needs."

"Communicate..." I responded. "I thought these so-called Greys were telepathic. How did they manage to talk to them?"

"It was indeed telepathic communication they had with the beings, and they revealed that they were more like time travelers than space travelers. Although classified as a type of Grey, these beings were not 'aliens.'"

"I'm not following you."

"These Greys were once human beings. They'd changed in the future due to a different environment. Over the course of centuries, human beings went underground because of a devastating future, then had drifted to explore the stars and now looked very different from us."

"So, where did they come from now?"

"The future human beings had arrived from a small planet about fifteen light years from Earth, and they used Looking Glass Technology to travel back in time. While their home system was real enough to them, it was only a potential reality for us."

"So, the captured Grey came from the future?" I replied.

"Yes," said Lazarus. "A future we created because of the Looking Glass." The military learned from their captive that he came from 45,000 years in the future. They later learned of another group that are from an offshoot time and came from 52,000 years in the future. These groups were labeled the P-45s and the P-52s."

"What's with the names?" I asked.

"The terms were an abbreviation for 'Present + 45,000' or the 'Present + 52,000 years.'"

"So, future humans look like Greys?"

"Not all future humans look like Greys, and not all Greys are human. A third group of future humans was discovered and called P-52 Nordics. These did not look like the Greys, but looked more like present-day humans. Now understand I am quoting this from someone else. They are a race of human that are very large, with large blue eyes. Compared to the other two groups, this is a very spiritual race."

"OK, wait a minute," I interjected. "Why did the P-45s and P-52s come back in time?"

"The P-45s had returned to find a solution to their poly-neuropathy, which had resulted from an apocalyptic past and excessive cloning. The P-52s, however, had returned to warn humanity about how the Looking Glass Technology could cause catastrophic harm to the timeline."

"How did you learn all this stuff?" I asked.

"This information was revealed by United States Navy Captain Danny Benjamin Crain, Ph.D., who was part of the Aquarius-J-Rod Team 6. He later fell out of favor with the military after he befriended a captured non-Nordic P-52 extraterrestrial and helped him escape back home to rejoin his family."

"Wow, really? So the extraterrestrial had a family waiting for him on his home planet?" I said with a smirk.

"Why does that surprise you? Love is a constant throughout the universe."

"So, getting back to their appearance...Were the changes in their physiology due to changes in their atmosphere and environment?"

"It's complicated," Lazarus stated, "but this is what I've been told. After the apocalypse, a group of surviving humans stayed underground. They shrunk in size and grew larger eyes to take in more light. Eventually, they migrated to Zeta Reticuli. This group later became the Greys that we call P-45s, not to be mistaken for the Orion Greys, who are true Greys. From what I understand they are taller and some of them are said to be working with the Reptilians. Now this is where it gets complicated. We're not sure if the P-45s are from the same timeline or a different timeline. It seems that another group left the Earth soon after and traveled to the moon, then to Mars and other star systems. This group later became the Greys that we call P-52s. There was also another group, part of the P-52s, who is said to have gone to the Pleiades with help from an ET race out that way. They flourished physically—developing large statures, as well as achieving spiritual depth and awareness. These became the P-52 Nordics."

"So I have a question," I replied. "Was it this so-called Secret Government that covered up the UFO crash at Roswell?"

"Actually, this was the beginning of the so-called Secret Government," Lazarus explained. "After the Air Force discovered how the black box from the Roswell crash worked, President Roosevelt created the Interplanetary Phenomenon Unit (or IPU), placing General George C. Marshall in charge. All IPU records were transferred to Project Bluebook, run by the Air Force. Later, President Truman gave the Air Force permission to form a group called MAJIC, which stands for Military Assessment of the Joint Intelligence Committee. MAJIC, made up of 12 military and political operatives known as MJ-12, inherited the black box information and went on to initiate Project Looking Glass. Later still, when the NSA allegedly took over MJ-12, the group was renamed Majestic-12."

"So I have another question. How did the Illuminati figure into becoming part of this Secret Government?" I asked.

"The Illuminati is a secret organization that has been around for centuries. Although rumors would say it is made up of a Reptilian race of ETs hell bent on controlling the human race, I would believe otherwise and say it is just a club for the wealthy elite trying to control the human race. But then again I could be wrong! From what I understand, the Majestic-12 received unlimited funding from the Illuminati because there was a potential to better control the human race and to make money from back-engineering this new off-world technology. The Majestic-12 and the Illuminati realized the benefits of working together, so there was a merging of the two. Sadly, this Secret Government is beyond all laws. Today, its technological power outstrips the civilization we live in. From their perspective, all the rocket science behind the Apollo missions is actually archaic.

"Their power arose as a combination of various factors. For one thing, they had unlimited funding to build their facilities and to hire the most intelligent scientists and technicians on the planet. For another, they made treaties with extraterrestrial groups like the P-45s. These treaties allowed the P-45s to abduct United States citizens for long-term genetic research to find a solution to the extraterrestrials' peripheral neuropathy. In exchange, the Secret Government obtained advanced technology."

"What advanced technology did they acquire?"

"I only know a little about their top secret projects. What I do know is that they have learned how to teleport individuals to the moon and Mars, build anti-gravity saucers called ARVs, or alien reproduction vehicles, and are now experimenting with time-travel machines, including the Looking Glass Technology."

"The question is, how did they manage to keep things so quiet from the public?"

"Often they used criminal methods to silence whistleblowers, like blackmail, intimidation, mind-control, and murdering those who broke their oath of silence. They also outsourced work to private aeronautical corporations to avoid keeping government records."

"So, was the movie Contact accurate about Looking Glasses? And are shows like the mini-series Taken by Steven Spielberg accurate about abductions and government secrecy?"

"You have to allow for some inaccuracies. For instance, in Contact, the scientists figured out how to construct the Looking Glass Technology based on messages encoded in radio waves received from the extraterrestrials. In reality, the P-52 met with President Eisenhower in 1954 to warn humanity about how the Looking Glass Technology could cause catastrophic harm. Also, in the movie, the Looking Glass Technology was restricted to only two constructions, but under MJ-12, more than fifty Looking Glasses were built over the years and used by the financial elite to control global events. As for Taken, that was fairly accurate in depicting the extent the government officials went to maintain secrecy."

"There is something I don't understand about this time-travel thing," I said. "In the movie Back to the Future, traveling back in time changes things. When Marty McFly accidentally prevented his parents from meeting in 1955, he put his own existence at stake. So when some of these extraterrestrials died after crashing in the past, didn't it affect their family line?"

Lazarus chuckled. "It would seem so, based on Newtonian logic. But according to the New Physics, the Grandfather Paradox nullifies that possibility."

"What is the Grandfather Paradox?"

"Timelines are complex phenomena because they are not as simple as a single line of causality moving forward from the past to the future, or moving backward from the future to the past. Instead, changing the course of a timeline will result in the creation of a parallel reality. For instance, if you were to travel back in time to kill your grandfather, you would not disappear into oblivion. Instead, at the time of your grandfather's death, another timeline would be created where you would still exist."

"Oh, I see," I said, pausing to consider the implications of what he'd just said. "But, surely, the extraterrestrials came back for a reason other than scientific curiosity about experiencing the reality of time travel."

"While the P-45s came back to discover how to save their own species from the neuropathy associated with the apocalypse that drove humans underground, as well as cloning methods that were making it impossible to reproduce and keep their race alive, the P-52 J-Rods and P-52 Orions time-traveled to warn humanity about the amplifying effects of using Looking Glass Technology to create artificial star gates. They advised the dismantling of these devices because they were the cause of the cataclysms that destroyed the planet."

"Did it happen?"

"According to whistleblower Dan Burisch, this has occurred. He also said that the last data collected from one of the Looking Glass devices showed that the possibility of catastrophe was averted by a probability of 85 percent."

"That's good to know. I didn't realize that my abductions were based on permission from the U.S. government, or that these ETs were responsible for sharing devices as sophisticated as the Looking Glass Technology with us."

"Based on my connection to the Angelic Realm, I can tell you that your abductions, Stan, were not by any of these three groups. Instead, they were by another group of Orions who had no earthly ancestry! The race itself was aggressive and somewhat warlike, not a very nice bunch to be around, but a percentage of them realized the error of their ways and have split off to become enlightened. They may even have an Angelic connection. They did not originate from the Earth. They are beings native to a system light years past Orion. These have been referred to as the True Orions, or the Priestly Orions, to distinguish them from the P-52 Orions, who came from our alternate future and look like us. The True Orions work with a faction of the Small Greys who are benevolent. They also seem to be working with the Angelic. All these groups are trying to undo the mess created by the Looking Glasses."

"I'm confused," I replied. "Now there are different Greys?"

"Yes," said Lazarus, with a look of confidence. "There are P-45 Greys, who are us in the future on one timeline; there are the P-52s or J-Rods, who are us in the future on another timeline; and then there are the ET Greys—some are good, some are not, and all look somewhat similar. Now that we are in a new timeline, however, it looks as if we have avoided an apocalypse!"

It was almost too much to believe, but it seemed to fit the information I was given by the ETs that Lazarus now called the True Orions. If I wanted to dispute this, where would I even start?

I sighed. "It's good to hear that disaster has been averted," I said, staring out of the window at the street. Watching a mother in a tracksuit walking with her two little daughters on the sidewalk, I found it hard to believe a top-secret time-travel device would have ended all life on earth.

"We may have avoided one calamity, but may not be entirely free of another one heading our way," commented Lazarus, ominously.

"What do you mean?"

"Although I think we're finished with Timeline One, I'm not sure we're completely done with the dangers posed by Timeline Two. All I've described so far are the dangers associated with Timeline One."

"Great," I whimpered, my head resting on one hand. "Now you're saying there's more?"

Chapter Thirteen

Timeline One

"In Timeline One, the Looking Glass Technology created the end of the world. Since our solar system moves through the galactic plane of the Milky Way every 26,000 years, the creation of the artificial star gates by using Looking Glass Technology would have allowed tremendous forces to ravage the earth. Star gates are wormholes used to travel through time-space."

"You're talking about natural disasters? Earthquakes, floods, tsunamis—that sort of thing?"

"The Illuminati were going to blame the apocalyptic disaster on a Mayan prophecy and they were going to use the ancient Mayan calendar foretelling the end of civilization on December 21, 2012 as their backdrop!"

"So do you believe in this Mayan calendar stuff?" I asked. "It is plausible that they somehow had insight as to what was going to happen?"

"Plausible," Lazarus said, "but inaccurate. First of all, the Mayans likely inherited the calendar from a preceding Mesoamerican culture, and the calendar is not as accurate as some have claimed. It is not even as accurate as the one introduced by Julius Caesar in 45 B.C. Ironically, when these doomsday prophets talk about the

Mayan calendar, they always reference and show pictures of the Aztec sun stone instead. But the Maya were not the Aztec."

"No kidding," I said with a smirk.

Lazarus chuckled. "There is still much debate over what the Mayan calendar is really trying to say, but according to a newspaper interview with Jesus Gomez, head of the Guatemalan confederation of Mayan priests and spiritual guides, 'There is no concept of apocalypse in the Mayan culture. The Maya think Westerners are off their rocker!' Despite this, some of these so-called New Age gurus, and I won't mention any names, keep saying there will be an apocalyptic event on December 21, 2012, and all because an inaccurate Mesoamerican calendar comes to the end of its cycle!"

"Maybe the Illuminati set this whole thing up," I said.

"You're probably right," Lazarus replied.

"But weren't the Illuminati worried about their own skins?" I countered. "After all, money can't buy everything, and mortal power can only go so far."

"Since the Illuminati had foreseen the disaster using Looking Glass technology, they had already invested billions of dollars to escape from the catastrophe by hiding in tunnels that run hundreds of miles underground. [See following page]

This labyrinth of tunnels was kept secret from the masses and was built rapidly. These underground survivors would leave the earth after 7,000 years, travel to the Zeta Reticuli star system, and become the P-45 and the P-52 Greys. However, not everyone on the surface would perish, and these survivors would leave the earth in 5,000 years, travel to the Orion star system, and become the P-52 Orion Nordics."

"It's a good thing that they decided to listen to the extraterrestrial warnings and dismantle the Looking Glasses," I said. "But how did they know the future version of us was telling the truth?"

"Actually, they had two sources of proof that verified this. One, of course, was what they saw for themselves in the Looking Glasses.

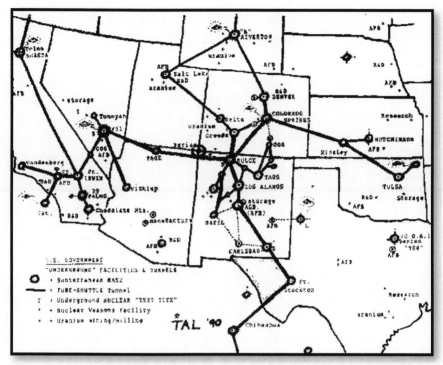

This is supposedly a map of U.S. Secret Underground Tunnels. One of my intelligence friends gave this to me. He got it off the Internet and said it was fairly accurate.

The other was a different device called the Chronovisor, which allowed a person to see into the past or the future."

"What is the Chronovisor?"

"It is another technology that was created by physicists at the same time the Looking Glass Technology was being built. The CIA took over this invention and absorbed it into a program called Project Pegasus."

"How did you learn about it?"

"From another whistleblower, Andy D. Basiago. According to him, by 1968 the CIA had learned how to efficiently teleport individuals to the past and future. They were able to retrieve artifacts and bring them back to our present time. Additionally, they were gathering information by propagating holograms of past and future events using the Chronovisor. It is not accurate to depict this as a time machine, per se, as the viewer does not go anywhere, but instead views past or future events on a screen, much like a television set. The technology is actually said to be Atlantean, and comprised of electromagnetic discs and an array of crystals."

"So this was not back-engineered from the extraterrestrials?"

"No, it was invented by human beings. In the early 1960s, Father Pellegrino Maria Ernetti confessed to François Brune, another Roman Catholic priest, that he had created the machine in collusion with twelve world-famous scientists, including Enrico Fermi and Wernher von Braun."

"What did it look like? Was it another huge array like the Looking Glass?"

"Actually, no. The device was described as a large cabinet with a normal cathode ray tube for viewing the received events. The time and the location to be observed could be controlled through buttons and levers. It was so precise that it could focus on specific people and track their actions in either the past or the future. According to Father Pellegrino Maria Ernetti, it received decoded images and sounds and could reproduce the electromagnetic radiation from past and future events."

"I get it. This device confirmed what the Looking Glass had already shown?"

"Yes. Using this device, the CIA informed Majestic-12 of the dangers of using the Looking Glass Technology. Majestic-12 responded to this warning and issued an order that all Looking Glass devices be disassembled by 2004. They got the U.S. Armed Services to side with their point of view, for the sake of saving the Earth. At least they hoped the Earth could be saved."

"I bet that went down well," I said sarcastically.

Lazarus responded with a smile. "True, the Illuminati were not pleased with this order and it caused a schism between the two groups. This was the same year that you were given the predictions by the aliens during an abduction experience. This change in Secret Government policy voided some of your most terrifying predictions."

"So the Illuminati reluctantly cooperated?"

"The dismantling of the Looking Glass Technology was not an easy task, because some of the global elite did not want to give it up. For instance, when George Bush declared that it was necessary to go into Iraq to stop a 'weapon of mass destruction,' he was not referring to a nuclear arsenal, but rather the Looking Glasses, and one was in the hands of Saddam Hussein, who didn't want to give it up. And now you know the real reason for the term 'weapons of mass destruction,'" Lazarus said. "The WMD weren't nuclear, as we were led to believe. It was the Looking Glass that we were after. And we got to it in time to shut the last one down. They've all been disassembled, which means that after 2017 they can potentially be reassembled."

"Hold on, hold on there," I objected. "Are you trying to justify the war?"

"Take a breath. Let me add this: Those in charge knew about the coming destruction. They were also in cahoots with the Illuminati who wanted to keep Timeline One. However, a group of the good Orion Greys, calling themselves the True Orions, were aware of all this and ended up using the administration to turn things around without their even knowing about it. Since the mainstream media, most of the politicians, and the general public were not aware of Looking Glass Technology, they did not know about the danger of creating artificial star gates. For that reason, a huge fuss was made about not finding nuclear weapons after the invasion."

"Lazarus, there is something that makes no sense to me. Although the global elite had an escape plan, I can't imagine living underground in a bunker as better than living a life of obscene wealth and unchecked power."

"Although many top members of the Illuminati are national leaders, corporate chiefs, and captains of finance and industry, they may not be the masters of their own destiny. Despite my own personal beliefs, it is said that they are overshadowed by an ancient alien race who helped them acquire all their earthly wealth and power."

"Who are these ancient aliens?" I asked.

"They are called Reptilians. They have been described as eight- to twelve-foot pterodactyloid-like hominoids. They are subterranean and supposedly have the ability to shape-shift. They are highly intelligent, immensely strong, and utterly vicious. Few people have seen them in their natural state. The only reported sighting in modern times is by Preston Nichols, who survived the disaster of the Montauk Project because they directly supervised that particular time-travel experiment. Since the Reptilians have been around for centuries, they have been included in our arts and literature. Certain archeological ruins have carved images of them. In mythological stories, they are described as dragons, snakes, and horned devils.

"They say that along with the bad Orion Greys, the Reptilians have ruled this planet for thousands of years. They've passed on their domination from generation to generation through the intermarriage of monarchies over the course of thousands of years. The royal bloodlines arose as a result of these aliens coming to the planet several thousand years ago and mating with human beings.

"Today, it is rumored that the Illuminati control the masses of humanity behind the scenes with the help of the Reptilians through political, economic, educational, and religious systems. Since most of the media, education, and entertainment industries are controlled by them, it is almost impossible for people to discover anything other than what the ruling classes permit.

"According to researcher David Icke, who has spent years investigating the Reptilians' influence on Earth, the purpose of the secret societies is to cement the bond between the Reptilians and their human devotees. It is only when you reach these higher levels of these secret societies that you find out what is really going on."

"So what about the Illuminati. How did they get involved?" I asked.

"The Illuminati was founded in the 1760s by a German intellectual, Adam Weishaupt. He organized the Illuminati with the help of the wealthy elite, who were said to be Reptilian and who provided liberal funding for the promulgation of everything necessary for complete control of the masses. They have infiltrated the Freemasons, as well as most of the other influential secret societies. They have influenced the outcome of governments around the world because these governments have become indebted to the International Bankers through the central banks of the world."

"I'm surprised that Majestic-12 managed to actually do some good for humanity, despite the Illuminati opposition to dismantling the Looking Glasses."

"I'm sure that most of the Illuminati saw the futility of destroying the world. There is also some conjecture that the intervention of the Angelic Realm and the avatars on Earth assisted Majestic-12 in successfully ending the threat of the misuse of Looking Glass Technology."

Despite all of this sounding like some chapter out of an L. Ron Hubbard book, I was enthralled. Somehow, something about it spoke to me, and I needed to know all I could find out. "So, what happened? What happened after Timeline One collapsed?"

Chapter Fourteen

Timeline Two

"After Timeline One collapsed, Timeline Two replaced it. Although the global natural disasters caused by the Looking Glass Technology have been averted, in Timeline Two we faced a possible horrible outcome and the world was poised to move into World War III. The Illuminati plan was to bring the extreme devastation to the world so that the creation of a New World Order appeared a viable solution.

"To make matters even more frightening, some say they were going to try and use the ET invasion scenario as an excuse. The upside is that the Greys, future human or not, would no longer be a part of screwing up the human timeline. It seems as if the current battle between the Illuminati factions and MJ-12 was carried out on a cosmic level, sealing off the wormholes of the Greys, both trapping them and preventing them from further exploitation of our future. So you see, your predictions from the Possum Lady serve as a baseline to let you know whether Timeline One has been avoided, and even sealed off. The information I have says that it has. Problem was, we still had to worry about Timeline Two."

At this point, Lazarus pulled a well-thumbed book out of his bulging briefcase. "In 1992, Dr. John Coleman published this book, *The Conspirators' Hierarchy: The Story of the Committee of 300.*"

He handed me the book, which he had marked with some Post-it Notes. "Read," he said.

I was shocked at what was in the book—it read like some Philip K. Dick dystopian nightmare:

"A One World Government and one-unit monetary system, under permanent non-elected hereditary oligarchists who self-select from among their numbers in the form of a feudal system as it was in the Middle Ages. In this One World entity, population will be limited by restrictions on the number of children per family, diseases, wars, famines, until 1 billion people who are useful to the ruling class, in areas which will be strictly and clearly defined, remain as the total world population.

"There will be no middle class, only rulers and the servants. All laws will be uniform under a legal system of world courts practicing the same unified code of laws, backed up by a One World Government police force and a One World unified military to enforce laws in all former countries where no national boundaries shall exist. The system will be on the basis of a welfare state; those who are obedient and subservient to the One World Government will be rewarded with the means to live; those who are rebellious will simply be starved to death or be declared outlaws, thus a target for anyone who wishes to kill them. Privately owned firearms or weapons of any kind will be prohibited."

I finished reading and tried to shake away the very thought of it, the possible reality that a sadistic ruling elite conjured up. "It gives me the creeps," I said, "thinking that some faceless people are planning to either kill me or make me a slave."

"You'll feel even worse after reading this part," he said, pointing with his skeletal fingers to another section of the book. In it, I read the apparent twenty-one goals of the Illuminati:

First, they planned to establish a One World government, a unified religion, and a single monetary currency.

Second, they planned to destroy all national identity and pride.

Third, they wanted to destroy all religions, especially Christianity, and introduce their own.

Fourth, they planned to introduce mind control and enforcement through technology, a process that Zbignew Brzezinski called the Technotronic Era.

Fifth, they planned to end all industrialization and create a zero-growth society.

Sixth, they planned to legalize all drugs and propagandize pornography as art.

Seventh, they planned to depopulate the large cities of the world, using the model the Club of Rome had successfully tested with the Pol Pot Cambodian regime.

Eighth, they planned to suppress all scientific innovation, especially that related to free, unlimited energy through fusion experiments.

Ninth, they planned to increase wars in developed countries and increase disease and famine in undeveloped countries to reduce the world population to 3 billion by 2050.

Tenth, they planned to demoralize workers by creating mass unemployment and encourage drugs and alcohol among the youth to destroy the nuclear family.

Eleventh, they planned to create one crisis after another to distract people from creating their own destinies and to increase apathy, with the Federal Emergency Management Agency (FEMA) managing the chaos.

Twelfth, they planned to increase new cults.

Thirteenth, they planned to increase Christian Fundamentalism and then tie it with the Zionism and encourage the Jewish people to think of themselves as God's chosen people.

Fourteenth, they planned to increase other fringe religious groups that could be classified as cults.

Fifteenth, they planned to encourage religious feelings throughout the world so that the various religions would become extremely radical, clash against each other, and cause violent outbreaks.

Sixteenth, they planned to create political chaos and economic collapse in all nations.

Seventeenth, they planned to take complete control of U.S. domestic and foreign policies.

Eighteenth, they planned to increase the power of supranational United Nations like the World Court, the Bank of International Settlements, and the International Monetary Fund and to decrease the efficacy of national institutions.

Nineteenth, they planned to destroy all governments by increasing corruption and destroying the idea of sovereign pride.

Twentieth, they planned to negotiate with terrorist organizations to encourage worldwide terrorism so as to increase a fearful population.

Twenty-first, they planned to destroy education in America, encouraging illiteracy and discouraging independent thinking.

Lazarus patiently waited for me to finish reading. I looked up and stared at him in disbelief.

"If you read the newspapers and watch TV, you'll see a lot of these already happening," he said softly. "Although it's been downplayed by the mainstream media, it's still there for someone to see the pattern emerging."

"They're not going to succeed," I said, suddenly angry. "It's outrageous. It's too big; they can't possibly get away with something this evil."

"They're doing fairly well, as far as I can tell," said Lazarus.

"How can you say they're succeeding? I mean look around you—the world looks fairly normal."

"The semblance of normalcy, based on a steady diet of media-issued lies and politically spun speeches carefully crafted on a teleprompter, has lulled everyone into a false sense of safety. When confronted with this type of information, most people react like you do—they simply refuse to believe it. They usually say something like,

'Oh, it's that conspiracy stuff. It's all hogwash.' Some even refuse to look at the information gathered by whistleblowers and dismiss it all without a second thought. They react the way they do because they are well-meaning people who don't understand the depth of evil in the world."

"It can't be true," I protested, thinking of getting up and leaving. Suddenly, I felt a surge of hatred for this messenger, considering him a threat. My disgust must have been obvious.

"I'm not the threat to your sense of safety and well-being," he assured me. "If you don't walk out on me, I'll show you some proof."

"What kind of proof?" I said defiantly.

"I'll simply summarize current world events to make my point."

"I'm listening," I said, feeling hoodwinked and resentful. He knew I was skeptical by nature, despite my own bizarre experiences with the ETs, and could only be persuaded with obvious evidence.

Seizing his opportunity, he began reeling off a list of things:

"First, let's talk about health. The plan to cull the population is unfolding through contaminated and poisoned food and water; for instance, fluoride is added in water to damage brain health; aspartame, a chemical used in rat poison, is commonly added as a sweetener in soft drinks; and arsenic, a poison, is in chicken feed.

"In addition, medicines and health measures actually promote illness; for instance, vaccines laced with mercury are continuing to be given to children despite a high statistical relationship between infant mortality rates and vaccination.

"Moreover, infectious diseases engineered in laboratories, like Avian Flu, Swine Flu, and Lyme Disease, have been proliferated to cause epidemics. In fact, more people died from the Swine Flu vaccination than from the Swine Flu itself.

"If this isn't enough, toxins are openly sprayed over the population by jet planes. Countries such as Australia, Canada, England, France, Germany, Holland, Ireland, Italy, Mexico, New Zealand, Scotland, Spain and the United States are spraying chemtrails from airplanes. Those exposed to low lying chemtrails have reported symptoms such as headaches worse than migraines, heartburn, heart conditions, cardiac arrest, flu-like symptoms, extreme fatigue, diarrhea, pain and swelling of muscles and joints, dizziness, nausea, stiff neck, nagging sore throat, and general malaise.

"Biochemist Will Thomas found the following ingredients after analyzing samples in the biological cocktail: Pseudomonas Fluorescens, a bacterium responsible for severe blood infections; Pseudomonas Aeruginosa, a bacterium responsible for attacking the respiratory system; streptomyces, a fungus responsible for infections in human beings; and a special bacillus found only in genetic engineering laboratories designed for creating a DNA restriction enzyme. What this allows, in effect, is gene splicing. A scientist can take a specific length from a DNA chain and transfer it to another organism, creating a mutation.

"Second, let's talk about wars. In Africa, the Middle East, and Central Asia, there is an increasing possibility of a big war engulfing the entire region as the U.S. engages in five simultaneous proxy wars with Iraq, Afghanistan, Libya, Pakistan and Yemen.

"Third, let's talk about economic collapse. In Europe, austerity measures are in progress in Greece, Spain, and Portugal. As these countries collapse, it will create a domino effect leading to the economic collapse of the U.S., the U.K., and Europe.

"And finally, let's talk about an example of intimidation. In the United States itself, governmental organizations like the Transportation Security, or TSA, was created in the wake of 9/11 to intimidate travelers by screening all commercial airline passengers; moreover, despite state legislators in Texas and Idaho protesting the molestation of men, women, and children, the TSA enjoys federal immunity.

"But," he continued, "this is just a mild form of trauma compared to the Monarch Project and the CIA's MK Ultra mind-control programs.

"Dr. Joseph Mengele, the Nazi doctor in Auschwitz, developed the trauma-based Monarch Project. He, along with 5,000 other high-ranking Nazis, were secretly moved into the United States after World War II in an operation called Project Paperclip. Kept discretely out of sight in U.S. underground military facilities, their methods were tested on American children kidnapped off the streets who were kept in iron cages. Eventually, after refining the methodology, they released the mind-controlled individuals to terrify the public. The list of mind-controlled serial killers includes Ted Bundy, David Berkowitz, Oswald, Timothy McVeigh, the Columbine shooters, Chapman, and Sirhan Sirhan."

I didn't know what to say. Like a flabbergasted plaintiff in a court case who had just been browbeaten by the opposing attorney, I could not make a case to defend my view that all was well in the world.

Unexpectedly, Lazarus smiled compassionately. "Before you slip into a deep depression, allow me to offer you some hope. We have not yet discussed what I have learned about the newest timeline, the one we're in right now."

"But all these terrible things are happening now," I squabbled. "How can we be in yet another timeline?" My voice was starting to quiver.

"Relax," he replied. "Let me finish. Without a doubt, Timeline One and Timeline Two must be avoided at all costs. Luckily we have help to do so from the True Orions and the Angelics.

Chapter Fifteen

Timeline Three

"In order to survive this second nightmare wave, we were going to get help from the True Orions and the Angelic Realm, or Celestials. But something unexpected is happening! There is a new timeline emerging and it is not because of the ETs *or* Angelic Realm but because of people."

"Wait a minute, back up," I said, totally confused. "So are you saying that humans are the cause for the changing timeline?"

"Yes," Lazarus replied. "But there is something you need to understand. Humans have no idea who they really are and what abilities they have."

"What are you talking about?" I implored.

The human race, without knowing it, has the ability to change quantum reality naturally. In short, they can manifest what they believe! This makes some nonhuman species nervous, including the Reptilians. More than that, humans seem to have a direct connection to Source. Some call it the Oneness, or God. In any case it is an unimagined conciseness. That is why remote viewing works no matter the distance. Humans just need to learn how."

"I remember talking to someone about remote viewing at a conference I was speaking at," I replied. "This guy was part of some covert military project that was involved with psychic research. There was even a movie made about him called *The Men Who Stare at Goats*. We were talking about my experiences when he told me that the military has four classifications for ETs:

1) ETs that like us that are non-psychic
2) ETs that like us that are psychic
3) ETs that don't like us that are non-psychic
4) ETs that don't like us that are psychic

"In talking, I asked him why some of these ETs that are psychic didn't like us. He said it was because of our potential. He said that even though the ETs are naturally psychic and are very efficient in communicating that way, most can only do so in short distances. Humans, on the other hand, are just learning, but they have the ability to communicate vast distances. And once humans learn to develop their abilities, the ETs are afraid we will be unstoppable."

"That makes sense," said Lazarus. "And I believe that the global elite trying to run the world, be it human or non, understand the ability humans have and are using it to their advantage."

"What do you mean?" I asked.

"By lying to the human race and keeping them in fear," he replied. "Humans have been lied to for centuries and are conditioned to believe what they are being told. In doing so they are manifesting what they believe. It's a vicious cycle. Even so, something is happening not even the Angelic Realm foresaw. Human consciousness got involved and is changing the timeline. With this new timeline it seems the planet will have a greater potential to move into global enlightenment, with the outcome being a possible paradise on Earth. If things continue on their current path, it will be a culmination of ancient prophecies of a Golden Age, a spiritual and intellectual renaissance for humanity unlike anything previously known in recorded history."

"That would be amazing!" I replied. "But when you say the 'Angelic Realm,' are you talking about angels?"

"In a word, yes," said Lazarus.

"OK, so how do they fit in now?" I continued.

"There are a lot out there that are completely focused on bringing harmony to all beings," he told me. "The True Orions, the Angelic Realm, or what some would call the Celestials, in addition to alien races like the Pleiadians, the Plejarans, the Andromedans, the Syrians, the Arcturians, as well as others who have the Celestials as part of their worlds and governing councils, are all working together to guide humanity to fully manifesting Timeline Three. The problem is they can only guide; they cannot get directly involved. It is an initiation of sorts. Humans must learn to do things on their own, like a child must learn to grow up. There is also another problem.

"Although Timelines One and Two have been observed in the time-travel devices, Timeline Three has not been viewed, so no one knows its final outcome, not even the Angelic Realm. So the big question is: Will the evil such as the Illuminati roll out with vigor and reckless expenditure of time, labor, effort and money to claim our world, or will the common man and woman awaken to their divine birthright and claim their world back?

"While humans are being guided by advanced aliens and spiritual beings, ultimately it is humanity's responsibility to free itself from the stranglehold of tyranny that is wrecking their world. How long will they continue to buy into the false promises made by politicians, the lies broadcast by the media, the distractions and myths propagated by the entertainment industry, and the brutal authoritarianism exhibited by government enforcement agencies?"

"Lazarus, what I am being taught through my experiences is that not one of us is as helpless as we may think," I replied.

"You're right, Stan. Humans are not as helpless as they're led to believe, even though they live in a world that can make them feel powerless every time they read, see, or hear the daily news. There exists a free defense that transcends government weaponry and requires only effort to use. It is that of the human mind. Sadly most focus on wealth, or the lack of it, as being the problem. Contrary to what many may think, wealth isn't their most important issue. Freedom is of the highest importance when the entire world is at stake. When freedom is taken away, so are life, liberty, and the pursuit of happiness. Freedom is the essence of all that humans are, and is the basic source of happiness. Anyone doubting freedom as a top priority should look at the history of the people of the old Soviet Union, eastern bloc countries and East Germany. They were born, lived and died in an oppressive, paranoid existence that's hard to grasp. Yet today, there exists a group of self-appointed world dictators that want to re-create that old style tyranny on a permanent basis for the entire planet, making it a prison planet without bars!

"Luckily humans don't have to accept that destiny, for the mind is a force on Earth that, when properly directed, is greater than all the dictators combined. Now let me explain. What has shifted the world from Timeline Two to Timeline Three is the morphogenetic field created by spiritual groups of different persuasion whose intention has been to experience enlightenment or tune into agape, unconditional love for all beings."

"I don't understand."

Lazarus continued. "Acting ethereally on various spiritual groups, the Celestials began to exert a profound effect on humankind using sacred geometry and meditation practices. Let me give you a few, out of many, examples:

"In the summer of 1993, physicist John Hagelin conducted an experiment in Washington D.C. to see what effect meditation had on lowering crime rate. For almost two months, 4,000 people meditated twice a day. Crime rates plummeted. Instead of the crime rate statistically going up by 25 percent based on a projected analysis of police reports, it fell by a 50 percent differential. Since the experiment was conducted by the founder of Transcendental

Meditation, Maharishi Mahesh Yogi, it has been called the Maharishi Effect."

"What is the Maharishi Effect?" I asked.

"Understand I am talking about how humans have a gift for changing quantum reality naturally. A Maharishi Effect is the phenomena of an increase in the consciousness coherence of any community. When 1 percent of a city practices meditation, it significantly reduces the level of crime in that city. Additionally, stock prices rise, pollution levels decline, and there is less unemployment."

"Can 1 percent of a national population decrease hostility between nations?"

"Yes, it can, because of the radiance effect of their consciousness coherence. It's the 1 percent solution. Here's how it works. If ten people, representing the 1 percent of a community, meditate together, the effect is greater than you would expect. If each person were to emit only one unit of harmonic energy, the total energy would not be ten but 1,000 harmonic units."

"I remember hearing something about this in one of my school science classes," I replied. "If I remember right, we added 1 percent of a crystal to a large vat of saline solution, and the entire vat became crystalline."

"Yes, you're getting the right idea. So if 100 people represent 1-percent of a population, it will create a hundred-fold effect, thus creating an effect of 10,000 units of harmonic energy."

"So I'm getting the feeling that the 1 percent solution is responsible for the creation of Timeline Three."

Lazarus smiled broadly. "In 2003, The Global Consciousness Project out of Princeton continued to study the effect of spiritual activities on consciousness coherence. In 2006, a meditation event in Colorado consisting of only 222 people created consciousness coherence.

"In June of 2008, an event called The Gathering of One—A Global Event was organized in Yellowstone, Montana, and 30,000 people on every continent of the globe, including Antarctica, joined them in creating the First Vibration of Peace. The purpose of this worldwide spiritual event was to end wars created by world leaders and the domination of the masses by the financial elite. It seems more than coincidental on September 29, 2008, the stock market crashed 777 points, an event that cost the global elite billions."

"My global predictions after this time also stopped becoming accurate," I added, beginning to brighten up.

"I'll give you one more example to drive my point home. In 2009, at the beginning of the summer solstice, the Celestials created sacred geometry around Idaho, Colorado, and Texas to coordinate with three sets of Solfeggio frequencies related to the tones of the Earth, the tones of Heaven, and the tones of Unity."

"Gentlemen!" said a voice, jarring both of us. It was Ping, standing over us, arms akimbo. "You have hardly touched your food, gentlemen," she scolded us.

Lazarus and I became aware of the room. Outside, the street lights were coming on.

"How long have I been talking, Stan?" asked Lazarus, somewhat bewildered.

"Too long, gentlemen," said Ping. "Maybe now I should bring you the dinner menu, too."

Then, with a twitter, amused by her own brand of humor, she began sweeping the bulk of our dishes onto her tray. Adroitly balancing the dishes, she disappeared back into the kitchen.

Waiting for our check, I had a flash of sudden knowingness.

"Lazarus, the shifting timelines, the machinations of the Illuminati, and the existence of ETs who are guiding us into greater consciousness need to be told to the world. It is our mission to encourage everyone to explore and expand their intuition, so we can collectively create a positive reality."

"Yes, the more people who can understand that we are not alone, and the more people who can tune in to the vibration of love, the more likely we are to experience a shift into global enlightenment; and the less likely we are to experience the economic collapse and wildfire-spread of wars that the New World Order is planning for us. But it is not *our* mission," he told me. "It is *your* mission. I am just a guide."

Suddenly as if on cue, something strange happened that caught me off guard. For a split second Lazarus was no longer Lazarus. His facial features, his eyes, and even his demeanor had changed. There was a regalness to what I was looking at sitting across from me, and whatever it was, it did not look human! Then, in an instant, the vision was gone. I sat there stunned.

With an amused look of concern on his face, Lazarus leaned over and asked, "Are you OK there, sport?"

Wondering if I had eaten something bad or if I was just overwhelmed by all that I heard, I began to doubt what just happened and I was not sure how to respond, so I ignored it.

"Yes, I'm fine...I was just thinking. So tell me more about my role in all of this again."

"Stan, you have had unusual experiences and you and I both know this wasn't by accident. People have come to trust you because you've collected a mountain of evidence to prove your experience with aliens is real. Now it's time to expand on what you have already begun with your book *Messages*, as well as your presentations. Sure, many will be as skeptical as you were at one time. But to those open-minded enough to do their own investigation, there is actually plenty of proof to validate what you're saying, even the most unbelievable parts of what I've shared with you."

"So, what you are saying is that my role is to share my experiences and encourage people to focus on oneness and the idea of unity consciousness?"

"Yes," he said, "so that humanity can deflect the potential of an Orwellian nightmare."

"Orwellian nightmare?"

"Orwell. George Orwell. His book *1984*. It's about a society ruled by an oligarchical dictatorship. It is a world of perpetual war, pervasive government surveillance, and incessant public mind-control. The political world is ruled by a political party simply called The Party. The individual is always subordinated to the state, and it is this philosophy that allows the Party to manipulate and control humanity."

"Got it," I replied. "I have not read the book but it seems interesting."

"You should," countered Lazarus. "It might help you better understand Timelines One and Two. People have to meditate and learn to pray for others, and act magnanimously toward one another. If the escalation of wars continues unchecked, and politicians and the media are tolerantly allowed to continue to lie about the real issues, humans as a race will indeed end up living the Orwellian nightmare, or worse, they'll all perish.

"And Stan," Lazarus continued, "if you can get this information into the hearts of freedom-loving people around the world, you may be instrumental in tipping the scales from a darkened world to a world where people actually live in the freedom they naïvely claim to have already achieved."

"I see," I said. "The alternative to a dystopia is a fabulous renaissance. While the military-industrial complex successfully collapsed Timeline One, it is now the role of the common man to deepen their own spiritual practice so that we can fully claim the Utopia possible in Timeline Three. When enough people are aware that our own government has been lying to us about the existence of ETs, and when enough people can connect with love for all beings, then the shift will happen." I paused for a breath, and then continued with a fresh burst of inspiration. "Each of us can contribute to saving the planet by choosing love over hate, peace over trouble-making, and compassion over mental, emotional, and physical violence."

"Exactly!" he burst with a smile.

It seemed as if I was starting to catch on. I had stuck it out and endured the most absurd account that I could possibly hear about why the world is the way that it is. Now if I could only get past the shock of it all. Unfortunately, but I suppose not surprisingly, something else just as startling awaited me.

Chapter Sixteen

The Elaborate Deception

May 2009

Lazarus received a call from one of the researchers involved with my case who had become a close friend of the family.

"Hello, John," he said. "I just got a call from Audrey. She asked me to give you a message."

"How do you know it was Audrey?"

"I don't for sure."

"Tell me what she said."

"She said that she wanted us to throw Stan a surprise book release party and to tell you that you are invited to attend. Then she also told us that Stan was to have an important visitor and that if Stan disappears for a short while, not to be alarmed; he'll be returned unharmed. And please don't say anything to him or he might not come."

"It sounds like Stan is being set up to be abducted," John said. "And I don't feel comfortable about this at all. I'm going to have to decline."

"I understand, but please don't say anything to Stan. If nothing else we wouldn't want to ruin his surprise."

After hanging up, John decided to take some time to mull over what he had just heard. Eventually he listened to his finely tuned intuition and decided that the real Audrey would not resort to such devious methods. It did, however, fit in perfectly with Black Ops schemes. He decided to call Lisa. He asked her if she would please visit him as it might not be safe to talk by phone. They set a meeting for the next day.

When Lisa arrived he told her about his conversation with our friend and his suspicion that Stan was being set up.

"I feel the exact same way," Lisa told him, tears welling up in her eyes. "I've been in tears for the past three days. Victoria told me that she got the same message and they decided to have the party for Stan."

"We all know that sometimes the Audrey calls are faked by those trying to hurt Stan. Apparently, the voice program used by the real ETs is a common one. The only way we can tell if it's from the ETs or not is if we find a way to tune into our own intuition and analyze the content of the message."

"Exactly—and this message seems to be more of a threat than a warning," Lisa nodded. "Sounds like something typical of the Black Ops."

"My feeling is that your intuition is correct," commented John. "An advanced civilization recognizes the importance of free will. This is a free will planet. Less intelligent, more atavistic beings choose not to recognize free will and get trapped in karma. Only the Black Ops would be interested in denying Stan the information he needs to make a good decision. It makes no sense that the ETs would want to deceive Stan..."

"I've spent three days arguing with Rick, Heidi and Victoria about why the ETs would never think in such devious and limiting ways," said Lisa, with obvious relief. "In a few words, you've clarified everything. You've justified my intuition."

Lisa got up and almost knocked Lazarus over as she hugged him goodbye. "Thank you for your wisdom. I'm so relieved to be able to make a clear decision. I'm going straight home to tell Stan everything."

Lisa pushed open the door. "Stan, we have to talk." Startled, I stopped buttering the English muffin I had just toasted in the kitchen. "Step outside," she commanded.

Oh, great. Now what the hell did I do? I thought as I was trying to remember what I might have accidentally done or said to upset her.

It was then that Lisa whispered, "I need to talk to you and I don't want us to be overheard by any wiretaps in the house. Let's go outside."

"Listen, Stan," she said. "Victoria, Heidi and Rick are throwing you a surprise book party on Wednesday."

"Why the hell are you telling me this? Why ruin the surprise?" I yelled.

"If you will stop yelling at me and let me finish, you will understand why." As Lisa explained the rest of her story, she confided that she had a really bad feeling that it was not the ET Audrey, nor the White Lighter Audrey.

I didn't know whether to be more upset at the fact that my surprise was blown or the fact that my friends would even allow something like this to happen.

"I'm not going to the party," I said firmly.

"That's fine with me. I have a very bad feeling about this. But if you change your mind, let me know. I need to call Victoria and tell her we're not coming."

"You know what, to hell with it. I'm going."

"Wait, you're what?"

"I'm going to the party. They went to a lot of work getting it set up, and now that I'm aware of what could happen, I'll make sure it doesn't."

Lisa was obviously hesitant. "Ah, you know it's probably the Black Ops, right?"

"That's what I'm guessing," I said with a devious grin.

***

No one knew that I knew about the fake Audrey call, or the surprise book release party. All they knew was that someone had to be with me at all times. So when we showed up I was forced to act surprised, and let me tell you, I milked it for all it was worth. (As planned, I was surrounded by a posse of loyal friends throughout the party, but knowing ahead of time why they were acting the way they did, I took full advantage of the situation to play a little game of hide-and-seek just to freak them out!)

The party was held at Victoria's house in a gated community. Her property spread out on the side of a fairly steep hill, nestled above the western part of a valley in the foothills of the Rocky Mountains. Scrub oaks surrounded her backyard, and just over a rocky knoll behind her property was a golf course. Any approach to her property would be easy to observe, so I felt somewhat safe.

As the party continued into the evening, we were out on the back patio drinking wine when everyone suddenly heard a noise in the scrub oak.

Inexplicably, flashes of light appeared in the undergrowth. In the past, such flashes indicated the appearance of an ET, like the famous recording of the "Alien in the Window."

More flashes followed, each one getting closer to the house. Everyone crowding the deck stood transfixed.

Out of nowhere a stone the size of a tangerine flew across the yard and landed on the patio with a thud in front of me. Everyone stared at the rock, astounded.

Then a second stone, this one as large as an orange, hit the deck. It bounced a few times before rolling to a stop.

"Wow," said my friend Mark, "this thing is really warm. It's almost hot. Who is throwing these things?"

Although a few of the men combed through the woods trying to find the hidden prankster, they found no one.

The party eventually started winding down and with no more flashes of light or stone throwing, it was apparent that there was going to be no abduction and no visitors. Most of my friends decided to go home, but a few who had visited from afar stayed overnight. The night was uneventful, with nothing out of the ordinary happening.

The morning came fast. One by one, we each grabbed a cup of coffee and shuffled onto the front deck to greet the warmth of the sun.

Sitting on the front deck with the other guests and talking about what had transpired the night before, I reflected: "Perhaps the ETs were throwing rocks to see our reaction."

It was then that we learned, to our surprise, that Rick Nelson secretly had two college physics students hidden in the scrub oaks with high-powered night-vision binoculars on the other side of the valley, watching over the house. From their vantage point, they could spy on anything that might try to access the house from the golf course or from the air. Using a video camera, they recorded the boisterous party on the patio, and then suddenly saw two three-foot beings with large heads peering into the windows of the opposite side of the house. Unfortunately, while they could see the ETs through night-vision binoculars, they did not have the sophisticated camera equipment to take pictures in the dark.

Rick was starting to describe what the physics students reported seeing when we heard the sounds of military helicopters coming over the hill off to the south. We could see that there were two of them flying very low, no more than a hundred or so feet above the ground. Beneath the helicopters, hugging their underbellies, was what looked to be an array of photographic equipment. Just as the helicopters flew right over us I raised my hand and gave them the one-fingered salute, just in time for a very bright flash to erupt from where the photographic equipment was located [see photo on following page].

I took a picture of this helicopter flying over us just before I picked up a rock to throw at it. You can clearly see the camera area just below the nose of the aircraft.

"Those sons of bitches just took a picture of us!" I yelled.

Just as I was about to pick up a rock and chuck it at the closest helicopter, Rick grabbed my hand and said, "Stan, knowing your luck, you would hit it just right and take down the whole damn thing, landing us all in jail."

His remark made everyone laugh, and although the Black Ops had attempted to intimidate us with their display of military might, we were overcome with spasms of laughter. I had the feeling that the commanding officers who would review the picture of us would not be amused with my salute.

The next day, my friend Mark called asking if I would go to a movie with him on Saturday. I felt bad because I hadn't spent much time with him over the past year, so I agreed to go. In retrospect, I should have been suspicious because Lisa showed no interest in joining us, and Mark twittered around like a nervous kid. But I was oblivious, despite Mark choosing to take the long way home and driving at an agonizingly slow speed.

By the time we got home, the sun was setting, painting the clouds from a palette of pink shades. Walking into the house, I noticed nothing unusual. Lisa was puttering around in the kitchen. "How was the movie?" she asked.

"It was great," Mark replied. Then he complained about the stuffiness of the house, asked for a glass of water, and suggested we sit outside because he needed some fresh air.

Without questioning a thing, I poured Mark and myself a glass of water and headed for the backyard. Stepping out onto the deck, I was greeted by a chorus of voices shouting, "Surprise!!!" Startled, I dropped my plastic water glass and within seconds the entire yard flooded with people who emerged out of their hiding places. A mob of people waved balloons with ET faces.

"Congratulations!"

"Congratulations on the book, Stan. You're number one! That's amazing!"

"Nice job, dude!"

People hugged me, pumped my hand, and ruffled my hair.

"Number one what?" I asked.

Rick Nelson smiled wickedly, a look of glee on his face.

"He doesn't have a clue," said Lisa.

"He probably couldn't handle it," said Victoria.

"Cute!" said Heidi, enjoying my bewilderment.

Lazarus hobbled his way over to me and handed me a piece of paper, "A gift for you," he said. "Congratulations, your book just went number one."

"Yeah," Lisa joined in. "You beat Zechariah Sitchin for the top spot. You took over number one!"

Overwhelmed, I shocked everyone by bursting into tears. A group swiftly came to comfort me. My friends' loving, comforting, and soothing words washed over me.

"People are actually hearing your story," said Lisa.

"They're finally beginning to listen to you!" affirmed Rick.

"Wonderful," Victoria chirped.

"It makes it all worthwhile," Lisa said, pinching both my cheeks.

"Way to go, Tiger," said Mark, punching my shoulder. He beamed with pride over having successfully made a complete fool out of me all afternoon long. *The little shit knew all along,* I thought.

Basking in the love of my wife and the warmth of my friends, I did not expect much more from the evening, but I was in for a surprise that would change my life.

The house was swarming with people—family, friends, and friends of friends—milling around the back deck. People sat in deck chairs with helium-filled ET balloons tied to them. Two large coolers on the deck were packed to the brim with soft drinks and beer, the kitchen refrigerator chilled the wine bottles, and a variety of dishes covered the dining room table. People were having a good time.

As the evening faded into night, it began to rain. The deck party moved inside and quickly filled the dining room and the garden level family room, a step below. People were pressed up against each other. Although I was in my element, remembering the past raves I went to and organized when I enjoyed the night club scene as a young man, others found it overcrowded and began to leave. Soon there where only twenty or so people left to enjoy the party.

Around 9 p.m. we were discussing the influence of Nikola Tesla on the modern world and how he used ancient Sanskrit terminology in his descriptions of natural phenomena. As early as 1891, Tesla described the universe as a kinetic system filled with energy that could be harnessed at any location. And suddenly a light flashed through the living room picture window.

Wondering whose car might be driving up the driveway, I looked out of the window and was surprised to see no car. Instead, I saw a small figure standing at the end of the driveway. It was a child, a beautiful girl with dripping wet shoulder-length blonde hair. She wore a grey-colored jumpsuit and stared directly at me as I watched her through the window.

"Hey you guys, there's a little girl outside just standing in the rain."

Victoria joined me by the window. "Oh, it's just probably one of the neighbors' kids."

Concerned about the drenched child standing there in the cold evening, I worked my way to the front door, but when I opened it, she ran down the street.

What parent in their right mind would let their child out this late at night in the rain in nothing but a grey jumpsuit? I wondered.

Although the number of people had thinned considerably by this time, the remaining gaggle of people had engaged in a conversation about when the government would publicly admit that they had plenty of classified documents about alien visitors.

Not being able to get the sight of the child out of my mind, I glanced out the living room window once again, and I was more than surprised to see that the little girl had returned. She stood there staring at the window smiling at me, indifferent to the pelting rain soaking her clothes.

"Hey, that kid's back," I said to Victoria.

"For Christ's sake, Stan, leave her alone," she snapped. "She's probably just a neighborhood kid curious about our party."

Under normal circumstances I would have listened but considering the situation I knew this was different.

Remembering that we lived on a street with no streetlights, I quickly searched for something to light my way but found nothing handy. Instead I grabbed the digital camera out of my pocket and made my way to the front door. Rick, sensing that something interesting was unfolding, followed me.

As I stepped outside the child bounded for the yard next door. In the darkness I used the flash of my camera to see where I was going. It was then that she suddenly peeked out from behind a tree; it was by chance that I snapped a picture of her.

There on the illuminated view screen of my camera glowed the face of an astonishingly beautiful child. I knew then and there that the child was not fully human, and if there were such things as angels I was no doubt looking at one.

"Stan, what's going on?" asked Rick, who had finally caught up with me. Overwhelmed I did not answer, but just stared at the camera viewer.

My camera had captured her impish grin. The girl had an almost porcelain, doll-like face with blonde hair framing a high forehead. More than that it was those eyes, those amazing almond-shaped eyes, too large for a normal human, slanting up at the corners at an angle—the irises were this incredibly deep blue color, almost violet. The beauty of her young face left me spellbound.

"Stan? Are you alright?" Rick asked, still gasping for breath.

I showed Rick the view screen.

"Where is she?" he gasped.

Although there were few places to hide, the girl had completely disappeared. Rick guided me back into the house, and as soon as we stepped inside he announced, "I want you all to see the picture Stan just took."

Everyone surrounded me as I showed them the picture. People were overwhelmed by what they were seeing, as if pure love was emanating from the picture itself. Some had tears in their eyes as they shook their head in disbelief.

Heidi whispered to Victoria, "I don't think I've ever seen anyone so beautiful. She looks like an angel."

The almond-shaped eyes of the little girl glowed of youth with an ineffable softness in her glance.

My friends urged me to upload the image onto the computer so we could get a better look on the big monitor. Alejandro and Rick followed closely as I took the camera downstairs to my office; just before we reached the office door, the camera beeped and the picture disappeared. I stopped abruptly and Rick and Alejandro bumped into me. I was crushed.

"It's gone!" I choked.

"Did you delete it by mistake?" shouted Alejandro.

"No! I didn't even touch the damn camera. I was just carrying it in my hands."

"Impossible," Rick stammered.

Two minutes had passed and we were still arguing about what had just happened to the picture when suddenly our phone rang. Alejandro grabbed it and handed me the cordless handset.

"Hello?" There was no answer. I rushed into the family room to break away from the noise.

"Hello?" I said again, pressing the phone tightly against my ear, trying to create a seal with my cupped hand.

Still no answer. Glancing at the caller ID, I saw that the number of the caller was my own home number.

Then I heard a soft, childlike voice answer, "Hello."

There was a long pause.

"Daddy," she said, "I love you. Don't worry. I'm all right."

The pure tone of the voice shocked me.

"I love you, too," I replied. "Hello? Hello. Oh my God," I said as I began to cry uncontrollably. It suddenly hit me why she looked so familiar: The angelic girl I just took a picture of was the child on the ship who hugged my leg so tightly. She was older now, but she was the same child, one of the seven I wanted to rescue.

"Stan, what's happening?" Alejandro demanded.

"What's the matter, honey?" Lisa asked.

"Hello?" I said into the phone, but only heard the dial tone.

"It was her," I gasped. "It was my daughter. The one in the picture."

Lisa held me while I sobbed.

Chapter Seventeen

Children From the Heavens

May 2009

Word of my hybrid daughter spread quickly from my support group. Rick, one of my avid champions, even told an acquaintance of his, a rabbi chaplain at the Air Force Academy in Colorado Springs. He became enamored with the implications of life from another world and decided to come and visit us on several occasions. He asked questions that caused me to consider the little girl's phone call from more than an emotional perspective, such as: How big is the house that holds all of God's children? Rabbi G., as we began to call him, fell in love with the notion that the immensity of God's love extended beyond anything we could understand. On one occasion, he even brought a white teddy bear to leave for this new child from the heavens.

When we asked him how he expected her to get the teddy bear, he simply walked on the deck and placed it on a bench, sitting there as if in expectation of a newfound love. "She'll find it," he said matter-of-factly.

Ironically, despite my skepticism, he was right. The teddy bear waited patiently for a week and then disappeared, with no sign of anyone entering our yard. Rabbi G. chuckled with delight when I called him with the uncanny news.

Although Lisa and I tried to find a more mundane reason for the disappearance, like the cat dragging it away and hiding it in the corner of the yard, we remained stumped by the "abduction."

Lisa and I love company, and our yard is something that reflects that. Our house has a revolving door policy. If you have to knock, you're probably not yet a friend and don't belong. At the Romanek's, it's "Walk right in, sit down, kick your feet up, and enjoy yourself." That and the fact that we take pride in taking care of our house and yard is part of what makes the house so welcoming. Lisa loves showing off her flowers.

Every spring and summer our yard turns into a variegated collection of irises, snowballs, marigolds, and pansies. The aroma alone puts a smile on the face of visiting guests. Lisa insists that planting and weeding make her happy and gets rid of stress. So, what makes her happy makes me happy. Unfortunately, I didn't always understand that.

It wasn't long before I learned not to ever touch the flowers. I had decided it would be nice to have a beautiful arrangement for the table from Lisa's garden—and I did this without asking. Long story short, it took an hour to calm her down, and I ended up having to replace what I took! I quickly learned that keeping peace in the house meant to simply not mess with her garden.

So imagine my shock to one day discover a little blonde girl hiding in our backyard...plucking Lisa's flowers.

It all started when I noticed the cats cavorting around the cooler that was left over from the book party. Their behavior struck me as odd. The more I observed their antics, the more intrigued I became by them.

Since I love taking pictures of our cats whenever they're acting goofy, I got my camera, opened the patio door, and began snapping away. As they pounced, I captured them in mid-air leaps and tumbling play.

But as I took a step toward the cooler, the flowers next to the deck, behind the cooler, began to rustle and a young girl with blonde hair bounded from her hiding place. Clutching flowers to her chest, she dashed through the open gate into the front yard.

"Hey!" I yelled as I chased her, intending to warn her about stealing Lisa's flowers.

I entered our front yard and spied the girl on the lawn next door. When she saw me, she headed for the neighbor's backyard, still clutching the flowers. Since the house was empty and up for sale, I thought I had her, but as I dashed through the open gate and rounded the corner, I heard a door slam. Bewildered, I searched the yard. She was nowhere to be found, and there was no place to hide.

I checked the back door that led into the patio, but it had been nailed shut. With my hands cupped, I peered into the house for any evidence of the little girl. As I was wondering how in the world she might have gotten in there, I was stunned to see a white teddy bear just sitting upright in the middle of the empty dining room floor.

"What are you doing next door?" asked Lisa, peering over our fence.

"You're not going to believe this."

"Try me."

I began to tell her what had happened and how I chased the little girl into the neighbor's backyard where she disappeared. Then I told her about the white teddy bear.

"I *know* it's the teddy bear that Rabbi G. left," I said excitedly, "but how did it get in there?"

"You're right," replied Lisa, "I don't believe you. But hold on, I'm coming over."

We both stood there transfixed, wondering how the thing got in the house. It had been vacant for a while and no one had keys other than the realtor and the owners who now lived in another state.

It was at that point that Lisa grunted, "Oh crap, I forgot we invited Lazarus and Lucie over for lunch. We've got to get back."

Not long after we got home, the doorbell rang and I immediately opened the front door.

"Looks like someone in the house has an admirer," Lazarus said with a smile on his face, pointing down.

A beautiful bouquet of flowers was neatly arranged on the front step. Looking closer we realized that they were the very same flowers that the little girl had escaped with.

We found these on our step shortly after I caught the little girl picking flowers in our backyard. Even though they were from my wife's flower garden, I thought it was a very sweet gesture.

"Where did those come from?" I asked.

"They were here when we arrived," said Lazarus with a shrug.

"Well, you won't catch me giving you any flowers," chimed Lucie. "I'm too damn cheap."

"You won't believe this...but I just saw this little girl picking them in our backyard," I said. "And when I chased after her, she disappeared."

"What?" Lucie countered. "You have kids delivering flowers? Aren't there child labor laws about this kind of thing?"

Lazarus chuckled as I carried the flowers inside and immediately took them downstairs.

"Stan, get your camera," Lazarus ordered. "And get a picture of these. Then when you're done, check the flowers with a black light to see if they fluoresce."

I found nothing out of the ordinary.

Then Lisa remembered that I'd taken pictures of the cats in the backyard when I first noticed the little girl.

"Let's see if you have anything on those photos you took in the backyard," she suggested.

I took this picture of my cats acting goofy just before the little girl stood up from behind the grill. It was after reviewing the pictures that I realized I had actually captured a picture of her.

Hooking the camera to the computer, we scoured each photo for anything unusual; then one of the photos caught my eye. I decided to enlarge it.

Right behind the cooler was a headshot of a young girl with reddish-blonde hair.

Notice her beautiful, oversize, slanted eyes. Oddly, after this picture, my camera stopped working.

She also had huge, blue eyes just like the blonde girl standing in the rain at my surprise book party, but this little girl looked different.

For one, she had reddish hair and seemed a little smaller than the first girl. We searched both properties for any more signs that the girls had been there but found nothing.

June 2009

A couple of weeks had passed when our friends Heidi and Sarah came to visit and to check out the photos we'd taken. They also wanted to check out the teddy bear sitting in the still-empty house next door.

Oddly, the camera that was used to take the picture of the first little girl no longer worked, so I was forced to buy a new camera. The new camera was an upgrade and had new features that would allow special shots and rapid focusing. So while the women were examining the vacant house in order to figure out how the teddy bear had materialized, I played with my new toy.

A typical Colorado afternoon rainfall had begun when the three women returned from their exploration.

"There's no sign at all of how anyone could've entered the house to put the teddy bear in it. All the doors and windows were properly locked," Lisa said as she walked past me to sit at the dining room table.

"Maybe they're using the vacant house temporarily while they're here visiting?" Heidi replied.

"Whatever they're doing, it makes no sense at all," confirmed Sarah.

Lisa decided to make something to eat. I asked Heidi and Sarah if they'd help me learn how to use the new camera. Eager to keep busy, both of the women followed me into the living room where I began practicing camera shots.

We took turns taking pictures of each other as we tried to figure out how the camera worked, but it was when Sarah was taking snapshots of me sitting in a rocking chair that I heard a noise just outside the window behind me.

As I turned I saw a young girl stand up. It seemed she had been crouching near the corner of the window.

"What the heck...There's a little girl outside!" I shouted as I bolted for the door.

Sarah followed on my heels. We both stood perplexed in the front yard.

"There she is," Sarah said, pointing to the neighboring yard.

We then watched as she bolted toward the back gate.

"We've got her cornered," I yelled, but when we exploded into the neighbor's backyard, we found no one there.

"Damn!" I yelled in frustration. "How do they do that?"

"I have no idea," declared Sarah. "There's nowhere to hide and the fence is too high to jump over. I don't understand how she can disappear in a plain backyard with a high fence."

Upon returning to my property, we went to the window where the little girl had been hiding. I noticed footprints in the wet mud.

"Wow," I said to Sarah, "look at those tiny feet. She was wearing some kind of weird boots."

"Can you make a mold of them?" asked Sarah.

"I can head over to the hardware store and get some Plaster of Paris," I confirmed.

When we entered the house, we let Heidi and Lisa know that the mysterious girl escaped and that she had left footprints in the mud.

"We gotta check the photos in the camera," Heidi bubbled. "Sarah was taking your picture right at the time the little girl stood up, maybe she captured something."

After I uploaded the pictures taken of everyone over the course of the evening, we discovered that Sarah did indeed take a picture of the new girl, now a third girl—this one also blonde but still different looking from the other two. [See top photo on opposite page]

As soon as the pictures had been uploaded, I headed to the hardware store. Lisa went to the kitchen for large plastic bowls to cover the footprints from the rain.

Once I returned it took less than twenty minutes to make a permanent cast of the little feet in the pansy patch. [See bottom photo on opposite page]

What's particularly interesting is that the pansies by the footprint stayed alive all the way through winter, in spite of sub-zero temperatures, ice, and snow. [See photo on page 180]

My friends and I were playing with a new camera when I noticed a little girl watching us from outside out front window. It was by chance that we captured her in one of the pictures.

We found her tiny footprints just outside of the window.

Where she stepped, the flowers stayed alive through the freezing cold of winter.

Fourth of July Party
at Romanek's
July 2009

Once the good rabbi heard about the new girls, he desperately looked for an excuse to get away from the Academy so he could pay us a visit.

Not being Jewish, I loved to pick his brain about his faith and respected the man deeply. Unfortunately, one of the last times we would see him was at our annual Fourth of July party. He brought a large one-foot by three-foot greeting card with the word "Welcome" splashed across the front. He immediately had everyone at the party sign the card, encouraging them to write welcome messages before he sealed it and placed it on the same spot he'd left the teddy bear. The night echoed with celebration and jokes about Rabbi G. and his Welcome Wagon mission.

At one point, we all gathered on the front lawn to toss ground spinners and other fireworks that more than likely fell into the "illegal" category. Rabbi G. had never really had the opportunity in his life to play with the forbidden. So I coerced him into lighting one of the ground spinners, only to have him yell, "What do I do now?!"

"Throw the damn thing! It's not a *frickin'* dreidel!" I yelled back.

His eyes went saucer-sized before he finally chucked the spinner far into the street, just in time for it to zip underneath a police car driving by.

"Oh crap," he gasped, as the spinner shot around underneath the unsuspecting deputy's cruiser. All six-foot-six of the rabbi shook as he covered his eyes, imagining what he was going to have to tell his superiors at the Air Force Academy as to why he needed to be released from jail.

"Are they stopping?" he whimpered under his breath. "What's happening?"

I laughed until I couldn't stand. The patrol car didn't even slow down. However, I couldn't miss the opportunity. "They're turning around! They're turning around!" I squealed. Resigned to his fate, Rabbi G. dropped his hands as if waiting to be handcuffed, only to realize I was thoroughly entertaining myself. He slapped me on the arm.

"God will get you for that," he told me, trying not to smile.

After spending the night, he checked out the giant greeting card on the deck before heading back to Colorado Springs. He seemed disappointed that it still rested on its spot. But like the teddy bear, it was gone within a couple of nights. And, sadly, so was Rabbi G. Last we heard he had been shipped off to the Middle East, which is sad...because he would miss the best parts of the ongoing story.

Chapter Eighteen

Intimidation

The appearance of the hybrid children caused quite a stir among my close tribe of friends. Question upon question erupted from all of us.

Why did they show up?

How did they appear and disappear so quickly?

Who was helping them with such advanced technology?

Were they living in the empty house next door, or using it as their entry and exit point in time-space?

What would happen when the world discovered that hybrids were interacting with humans?

The implications were far-reaching, with regard to humanity's enlightening contact with extraterrestrials, and foreboding, with regard to whether we were somehow being used to replace Earth's population with another race of beings. No matter what the reason, it would surely have an impact on humanity's future.

As we debated these questions amongst ourselves, we decided that everyone had to know about this incredible development.

The discussions took me back to my conversation with Lazarus in the restaurant. Perhaps the appearance of these girls was an indication that the timeline had indeed shifted, or maybe they were just here to guide us? In any case Lisa and I had several debates over the sudden appearances of the little girls. Lisa had legitimate concerns that the children might be used in an attempt to manipulate me. By instilling in me the fear of danger to the kids, I might be persuaded to keep quiet. She feared a hidden agenda. My instincts told me otherwise. The next question was whether or not the girls were indeed from me. The similar facial features more than their huge blue almond-shaped eyes led me to believe that all three girls were my hybrid daughters.

Since I had been invited as a keynote speaker to the Galactic Gathering Conference in Denver on the weekend of September 25, 2009, I decided this would be the perfect time to reveal this astounding piece of information to a large audience.

But the opposition was intent on discouraging me from sharing this information with the world, and I became keenly aware of the extreme measures they would go to intimidate me into silence.

Lakewood, Colorado
Early September, 2009

A few weeks before the conference, Lisa and I were invited to Longview High School, a progressive school in Lakewood, Colorado, to speak before teenagers in a class about the reality of paranormal phenomena. Since their teacher had invited me to present a discourse on the topic of UFOs, I decided this might be a perfect opportunity to see how young adults would react to the notion that children from space were visiting Earth. The teacher gave me permission to share my recently captured photographs.

On our way to the high school at the corner of Sixth and Federal, something exploded ahead of our van. Lisa screamed and I jolted back as a bullet hit the windshield. I hit the brakes, swerving back and forth, trying to avoid another shot.

I scanned all the mirrors, trying to detect a gunman in a pursuing car; seeing no one, I decided to pull over to the side of the boulevard. Lisa stared at me in shock and disbelief. We were puzzled over why the windshield had not exploded and searched the dashboard for the bullet. Eventually we found pieces embedded in the windshield right in front of my radar detector.

After Lisa and I calmed down, we decided not to let the Black Ops intimidate us and continued on our way to the high school, planning to visit the police station afterwards.

After choosing a parking space at the high school, I locked the van doors and looked around to see if we were being followed. We walked nervously toward the school building, half expecting to be mowed down by some unseen sniper hiding in the trees.

Entering the classroom, a comforting thought swept through me: The 28 young people staring at me were part of the future, open to hearing the truth that others were so determined to deny them.

I put a smile on my face, introduced myself, and talked about my recent encounters with the Secondary Reality, initiating them into a bigger world than they had imagined. As I spoke, a new surge of power and confidence filled me. Something deep within me told me that everything would be fine; our world would be ready to hear what I had to say, and these beautiful, smiling faces listening to me would carry on the message.

When I finished my talk, hands went up immediately. Although they had the usual questions about why Earth was being visited and why I was the focus of so much attention, they also engaged in a discussion about their own role in what this meant to our world. My eyes began misting as I listened to them discuss with each other the roles they could play in welcoming to our planet the races who were obviously here to help us, despite the recent spate of television shows and movies that portrayed all aliens as cunning and cruel. I knew better. There was good and bad everywhere. I suddenly remembered an old chestnut from the Bible: "As in heaven so on

Earth." I never thought about what that really meant until that very moment. I was sure there had to be good and bad aliens. The trick was telling them apart.

As the discussion began to wind down, many of the students shared their own experiences of spotting UFOs and how they had reacted with excitement rather than fear. This positive reaction was a surprise and filled me with pride and hope for the future of our own race.

On the way back to our van, Lisa commented, "What a day of contrasts. We went from fearing for our lives to sharing ideas that would illuminate the minds of our young people about other sentient beings visiting our world."

"After a day like this one," I reflected, "it makes it worthwhile to speak my truth in public."

A week later, something unexpected, bizarre, and absolutely wonderful happened. Not only would I find out that I had someone watching over me, but what I would learn would soon answer some of our most perplexing questions and put everything into perspective.

While on the phone with Heidi about an upcoming conference, a clicking noise interrupted our conversation, and then our voices echoed as if we were in a canyon.

"What's going on?" I asked.

"Sounds like someone is trying either to monitor our call or break into the line," Heidi observed. "Someone should get out their recorder just in case."

The experience with the various Audrey calls had us all prepared. Everyone had some sort of recording device sitting by their phone. One never knew if the call coming in was important so it was better to be safe than sorry.

"Damn it. Heidi, I can't find mine," I said in a panic.

We heard another click, and then a child's voice. "Daddy?"

"Huh? Did you hear that, Stan? Get your recorder."

"Yeah, I am. I'm getting it." I scanned my home office for my portable digital recorder but couldn't find it.

"I don't see it."

"OK, I've got mine," said Heidi.

"Then turn it on. I'm hearing the voice again, but I can't understand it."

Then the voice became clear. "Daddy?"

"Hello?" said Heidi.

"Daddy, don't worry. We're fine. It's too dangerous for us to be there right now. You couldn't protect us even if you wanted to. We didn't mean to interrupt your call, but we thought you should know...there are nine of us. Seven of the same, and two, each one with different. I am the oldest! I am Kioma. It means 'Trinity.'"

I held my breath.

"And Heidi?" continued the little girl.

"Yes!" answered Heidi anxiously.

"For you, my sister's name is Trilly. It means 'to shine.'"

A long pause followed; then the little girl continued. "Daddy, we know you are excited about your talk this weekend, but please be careful! There are some that don't want you to talk at all. Sorry for the bad connection. It's all we have for such long distances. If we get disconnected, it means..."

The voice became distorted.

"Hello?!" I shouted.

The garbled sound echoed back.

"Hello?!" tried Heidi.

Again, more distortion.

"Oh, my God! Go ahead, Honey. What?"

Silence followed and then the phone call ended.

"Wow...that's amazing," said Heidi.

"I can't believe that just happened."

"Honey," Heidi warned, "you are going to have to be careful about this conference."

"I know, I know. I will be. But what do you make of this call? It's so cool to find out the girls have names."

"Oh my God, oh my God! It's so wonderful to actually talk with one of the girls. It's so wonderful to know I have a daughter named Trilly. I hope I get to see her someday..."

We continued talking about what the call meant, on more than one level. After hanging up I replayed what the little girl said over and over in my mind. I now knew there were more than just Victoria and I involved with this hybrid program. Now Heidi, too, would play a role. The question was, Who *else* was involved?

After the initial shock wore off, I remembered a dream that Lisa told me about a few years before. In her dream she was visited by an extraterrestrial. She was surprised to see the ET holding a very small baby. He handed her the small child, and, watching her reactions closely, he presented her with a second baby. Lisa told me that holding two small babies was a piece of cake for her; she had given birth to her three-pound human twin daughters, April and Nicole, so she wasn't unnerved about holding these equally small babies. That is, until the alien tried to hand her a third baby. It made me wonder, *Was Lisa's dream really a dream? Or had she been shown three of the nine children? Was she too a mother of a hybrid child?* During that unexpected call, the little girl who called herself Kioma told us, "Seven of the same, and two, each one with different." Although the wording is a bit awkward, it sounds like she was trying to tell us that seven of the children were from one woman, and the other two children came from two different women. Then I remembered back to 2003, when we lived in Nebraska, an incident with ETs by the side of the bed, being upset about Lisa's partial hysterectomy.

If I had it right, Victoria had to be what we jokingly call a "hybrid baby mama" to at least seven of the children. So, that would leave Heidi with one, and Lisa with one, and after all that had happened over the years it started to make sense. There were still so many questions, but questions aside, I had to get ready for this next talk.

Then I remembered the warning Kioma gave me about going to the conference. It seemed crazy, but my instincts told me to trust these benevolent, otherworldly calls. I began to wonder what dangers might lay ahead. If these people were desperate enough to shoot at me and Lisa, what else might they try?

Galactic Gather Conference
Denver, Colorado
Weekend of September 25, 2009

The intimidation picked up again when the organizer of the Galactic Gathering Conference received a phone call warning him that if he allowed me to speak, a bomb would go off at the hotel where the event was being held.

The conference organizer quickly alerted the hotel. The hotel security team, along with others, scanned the conference complex and found nothing. Playing it safe, they nevertheless decided to put a series of security precautions in place.

Lisa and I, the event organizer, and even the hotel manager had decided to make our stand. We refused to be intimidated into silence. Moreover, we were joined in our resolution by all the attendees, who were fully briefed about the threat.

As an added measure of precaution, Lisa and I decided not to stay at the hotel but at Victoria's house in nearby Littleton. Once we were finished preparing our vendor area at the conference for the next day, we returned to Victoria's.

Luckily, because we were concerned, in a hurry, and making changes off the cuff, we hadn't had time to unload our van when we first reached her place. Our suitcases and overnight bags were the only luggage we put in the house before heading off to set up at the conference, which turned out to be a good thing. We had returned to the house to find that her front door had been forced open with a crowbar. Then we realized that we couldn't get in because the intruders had jammed something into the door lock when they shut the door and had broken it off.

"Maybe they were trying to force us to stay at the hotel," Lisa suggested.

Refusing to be outwitted, Victoria used her garage door opener to let us into the house through the garage. We eventually gained access to the house and noticed the living room appeared untouched, but the guest room where we were staying had been ransacked. The bed was overturned, our luggage snapped open, and our clothes strewn everywhere.

"Perhaps they were looking for information about the children," speculated Lisa.

"It's a good thing we took all our documents with us to the conference center," I commented.

Without hesitation I called the person in charge of security for the conference. He worked for the sheriff's department, so I knew he would know what to do. He immediately drove over to check everything out. After making sure there were no devices in the house that might present a threat, he informed me that I would have bodyguards for the rest of the conference.

With everyone working together, the conference went off without a hitch—another triumph for those seeking to bring the light of truth to a dark world, and another instance of determination conquering fear.

After so many years of talking publicly about my experiences, I had become an old hat at doing speaking engagements and prided myself in being prepared for just about anything. It was becoming a trend, however, that whenever we reached an empowering smooth patch, the Universe would throw us another curveball. What happened next would change everything.

Chapter Nineteen

The Return of the Elohim

Early Fall 2009

I awoke suddenly, my heart racing and my adrenaline pumping. "What the hell was that?" escaped my lips. The memory of what had startled me awake was suddenly gone. It was still early in the morning; the sun was sending its first pink-tinged rays through the bedroom curtains. Just enough light got through to eerily illuminate the inside of the room as I struggled out of bed in search of a warm housecoat to put on. I couldn't shake the feeling that something strange had just happened. Still too groggy to remember much of anything, I went to the kitchen and poured myself a cup of coffee. The memory suddenly came flooding back like a torrent.

In my mind, however, I was having a hard time figuring out if what I had experienced was real or if it was some outrageous dream. Dream or not, what I remembered is that I woke up in the middle of the night because of a noise off to the side of the bed. When I turned my head to see where the noise was coming from, I was irked to see what looked to be a Grey standing by my dresser. Trying not to panic, I flipped over to get a better look and realized that whatever it was, it looked familiar somehow. Then it dawned on me: It was the ET I took a picture of—it was Grandpa. But there was something strange about what I was seeing; there seemed to be a faint blue glow coming from the being itself.

Slowly, as if not to startle me, it pointed at me and then at itself. I realized it wanted me to pay attention, so I nodded my head to let it know I understood. At that point the glowing Grey moved its hand to the top of its head and, just like in the scene from the movie *Cocoon*, it began to unzip itself. From the fallen-away skin emerged a very tall being surrounded by a blinding blue light. The bluish light was so intense I was forced to look away. Suddenly a voice, low and flowing, resounded through my head: *We use this first form because it is what you expect. We use it so it is easier for you. But this is who we really are.* That was all I remembered. Because most of my past experiences seemed a lot more involved than this, I assumed this was nothing more than a dream and promptly blew it off. Then something else happened that made me reconsider.

Three days later
At my house

Once again I woke up with the feeling that something strange had happened the night before. This time the dream was more vivid. I remembered waking up in the middle of the night because I thought someone was shining a flashlight in my eyes. That's when I noticed a really bright light leaking through the shades of the bedroom window. I shuffled down to the kitchen because I told myself I needed a glass of water. But really, I needed to check out what was causing the light.

Certainly the neighbor hasn't built a spotlight in his yard, I thought.

As I entered the kitchen, I realized the light was too bright to even be a spotlight. It seemed to come from everywhere. I began to wonder if one of the electric transformers had shorted out, but

I had to dismiss that thought because there were none near the house.

Pulling the patio door open, I walked outside. And there in the yard, just past the deck, emanated a blue brilliance coming off a being. The being looked to be about seven feet tall. At first I couldn't look at him long enough to tell exactly what he looked like because the energy was so intense.

"Don't be frightened," it said. "No harm will come to you. We are Elohim. We have returned. The children are important. You will be told more, when you are ready to hear it without fear. The children cannot stay here for now. Baby steps. It is time for you to wake and know who you are."

As my eyes adjusted I could see that even though the being's body was better defined it looked almost liquid. If one took the blinding light away, it had a humanoid shape. I assumed it spoke telepathically only because I never saw what could be described as a mouth. The voice didn't travel to me from across the deck and yard; instead I heard it as if he was standing next to me, softly speaking directly into my ear. As the tall being of light faded from view, a swooning dizziness enveloped me. I woke up in my bed the next morning wondering if this event, too, was a dream.

There weren't many people that knew about my experiences with the being of light. Just my wife and a handful of friends. So it wasn't until many months later, after Lazarus and I had the discussion at the Wonderful Dragon, that I decided Lazarus, more than anyone, might be able to help me figure out what happened.

October 2009

We decided to meet at Lucie's house. Luckily one of my good friends, Dr. Stanislav O'Jack, was in town and staying the weekend at her house. I met Stanislav, a well-respected clinical psychologist, through a mutual friend.

Considering what I had experienced, there were many times I questioned my own sanity. I had been looking for someone qualified to run some tests to see if, by chance, I had lost my marbles. As far as I was concerned, Stanislav was more than qualified for the job. After much psychological testing, it was a surprise to some to find out that I was not suffering from any mental illness. On the contrary, I had to be extremely stable to endure what I had experienced without losing it. Stanislav is one of the smartest and most enlightened men I have had the pleasure of meeting. I enjoyed my visits with him, so it wasn't long before we became friends. I was glad he was there.

While Lisa and Lucie were up in the dining room, Stanislav, Lazarus and I had decided to talk down in Lucie's den. I was in the process of discussing the possibility that my encounter with the being of light might have been a dream when we suddenly heard a high-pitched hum envelop the room. I got up to see if I could find the source of the sound. A millisecond later I felt something brush the back of my calf. Thinking it was a fly, I instinctively shooed it away only to realize there was nothing there. Both Stanislav and Lazarus were looking at me with puzzled looks on their faces.

"Did you see that?" Lazarus said as he turned to look at Stanislav.

"I did!" said Stanislav. "We need to document this."

As I stood there trying to figure out what in the world the two of them were talking about, Lazarus pointed down to the back of my calf. There on my calf was a series of six freshly formed, slightly bleeding holes in the shape of a perfect triangle.

"What in the world?!" I gasped.

"I watched it happen as you were standing there," remarked Lazarus.

It was apparent that it was more than a fly that buzzed my calf. The question was how it happened and why.

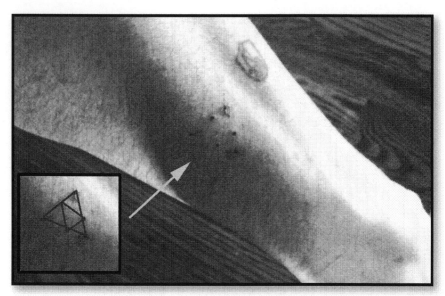

Photo taken by Dr. Stanislav O'Jack right after he and Lazarus watched these form on my leg.

Unfortunately there were no immediate answers. That's when Lazarus suggested it might be time for another regression.

"You've been resisting doing another hypnotic regression session for months. Don't you think it's time to contact Dr. Leo Sprinkle again?"

Leo isn't an easy man to contact. Being a believer in human interaction, he doesn't do e-mail, nor is he much for cell phones. Something deep inside encouraged me to use that as an excuse for not arranging the date. However, Lazarus isn't a man who is easily put off.

"Stan, I want to respect your decision. But try to understand that I believe there is an important reason for the encounter with the Elohim. Not to mention the marks that magically appeared on your leg right in front of us. Search within yourself and you will see if I'm right about this."

Lazarus had a way of putting things into perspective and pointing out the obvious. It wasn't long before I found myself once again sitting in a recliner waiting to start a session with Dr. Sprinkle. The unimaginable was about to be revealed.

Chapter Twenty

Answers: Regression Nine

March 7, 2010

In the days before the regression, my anxiety level rose dramatically. I was used to having my friends with me for moral support. However, this time would be different; it would only be me and Lisa, Leo, Lazarus, and Lucie. We had agreed that there would be no audience at this session. Lazarus had encouraged me to keep it small—the less interference the better. It was our turn to ask questions. Lisa and Lazarus had put together a secret comprehensive questionnaire ahead of time. We all agreed that Leo had to "OK" every question beforehand, which he did. I was not allowed to know what the questions were. The number of questions they had come up with was quite large, and because of time restraints we all agreed to stick to the questions on the questionnaire, unless something of a surprise turned up.

   With cane in hand, Lazarus began to hobble around me, placing stones in a formation around the recliner. As I looked to see what he was doing, I noticed it was the same set of stones he used the last time he guided me into that trance-like state. Noticing the questioning look on my face he told me, "I want to make sure that you aren't interfered with and that the information we get is clear." Lazarus knew I had never been comfortable with the entire notion of Grandpa coming in through me during the previous regressions with Leo. I simply did not trust this thing at all. He then told me that the sacred stone formation would keep out any negative influence and that included anything with an agenda.

As I was sitting in the recliner, waiting for everyone to get settled enough to start the session, I asked Lisa to make sure the video camera was running.

"You ready?" asked Leo in a calm voice.

"Sure," I quipped nervously.

As Lucie pulled all the blinds shut and turned on subdued lighting so Leo could read if necessary, she attempted to lessen my fear.

"Oh, Stan, pull up your big boy panties and get over it. You're such a girl." That made me laugh and I began to relax. All the phones were turned off except the phone in the upstairs master bedroom. Lucie had gathered the three remote handsets from around the house and hid them in her bedroom, shutting the doors so as not to interfere with the recording. As I lay back in the large Lazy-Boy fullback chair, I noticed the tension on everyone's faces, especially Lisa's. We had been through so much together. Here was one more episode where she and I were about to step into the unknown once again. Once Lisa made sure everything was turned on and recording, she sat down. The session started.

As soon as Leo's voice repeated the technique he had used before, my mind went blank. No one knew what to expect. Once I had been induced into hypnosis, Lazarus presented the three pages of questions for Leo to explore.

As Leo finished setting the conditions to my unconscious, there was a sudden movement that caught everyone's attention. It was a movement they had all seen before. With my eyes remaining closed, my head lolled back and forth as if searching for something. This was the telltale sign that another consciousness was now in charge.

Leo: Greetings.

Stan: Leo. *(Broken voice.)*

Leo: Yes. Hello. Welcome. *(Smile of expectation on his face.)*

Stan: Hello.

Leo: May we ask questi--?

Stan: Yes.

Leo: and allow the information to flow through Stan?

Stan: Yes. *(Said with emphasis.)*

Leo: Good. We have many questions that we would like to ask, and we hope that you are willing to consider them. John and Lisa have put together these questions that I would like to ask you. Thank you very much for your consideration. We noticed last spring that there were six marks that were left on Stan's ankle...three points. There was some question as to whether he had been abducted or not. Can I get any information on that?

Stan: Yes. Mmm...word...to test...to test...a test. Mmm. We were curious about his illness...to determine if it was our cause or not.

Leo: Where was this test done?

Stan: Here.

Leo: In his house?

Stan: No. Here.

Leo: In Stan's body?

Stan: *(Mumbles word...mmm...word...mmm.)* Humans do not understand. Mmm. Instantaneous. It can appear without you knowing. It did not take long. Just a test. *(Said without emotion in monotone voice.)*

Leo: And what did you find out?

Stan: We did not cause his illness.

Leo: Can we find out what the cause of the illness is?

Stan: It is from someone else. We believe it is from other human, not us. They want to make him ill so he keeps quiet.

Leo: Can you tell us how they are doing this?

Stan: Mmm. We do not know as of yet. Mmm. We believe it is various things. It is...mmm...word...what you call...possible pathogen and...mmm...other things. Mmm. Also psychic...psychic. There are multiple levels of attack. But, it will not work.

Leo: So are the pathogens in his house?

Stan: Mmm. There are some. Yes. He is being attacked. The family is being attacked. More than that, Stan's illness is from...mmm...a substance that has been introduced into his system that has offset his metabolism. *(Mumbles muh..muh...word...metabolism, metabolism, metabolism.)* And...mmm...word...mmm...mmm. There are multiple things and we believe that most are caused by...mmm...others, not us...Government.

Leo: Is there anything that can be done to help his health?

Stan: Mmm. Yes. He must continue seeing...mmm...physician, physician. We cannot get involved. We are not allowed. We have done so in the past and have been...*(Mumbles word... mmm...word.)* Mmm. We can no longer do so. We can guide, only guide.

Leo: Can you tell us where the reprimand came from?

Stan: It is not important.

Lazarus: Oh. The reason why we are asking is because we are trying to bring this information to the world. And if we understand it…

Stan: *(Interrupts)* It is not allowed.

Lazarus: OK. Umm. When you say, "we"?

Stan: Council.

Leo: You are a member of a council?

Stan: That is correct.

Leo: Are you able to speak about the make-up of the council—the actions, the philosophy of the council?

Stan: There are…word…types. *(Mumbles different…different… different types.)* Some higher, some lower vibrations. Some physical. Some between physical. *(Moves right hand in a "so-so" back-and-forth motion.)*

Leo: So there are various frequencies, various vibrations?

Stan: Yes. Densities. Densities. You may call them densities: Third, fourth, fifth densities.

Leo: And do they show themselves as entities, as beings?

Stan: It is easier for fourth density to show themselves as three density beings. It is harder for fifth density beings although we do accomplish it sometimes. *(Begins flexing right hand and brings it up in front of his face as if he is "looking" at it, but his eyes remain closed.)*

Leo: Thank you. So have there been any further abductions since last time I was here?

Stan: Visitations.

Leo: Very good. And who were the visitors?

Stan: You know this. (*He says this abruptly. Somewhat irritated.*)

Leo: I may. But it is better so that we can record it because of what we need the information for.

Stan: You may call them Orion...Orion. They are different types of Orions. These are fourth density...higher level.

Leo: We have been given indications that there are two different kinds of Orions. Is this correct?

Stan: There are more than two. (*A bit as if "you" should know this.*) There...are...in the Orion system is...mmm...word...three...three parts...different densities. They are...word...(*Hand gesture of one...two...three segments, as if slicing each segment with his hand.*) Word. (*Deep breath.*) There are multiple civilizations within this alliance...not alliance (*Shakes head no*)...word... they are separated but the center is an overlap. There are... mmm...underlords. (*Mumbles your word...underlords.*) There are underlords. They are higher density Orions...true Orions. Mmm. Blue eyes...blue eyes are the higher density. They are...mmm... word...priests...mmm...fourth density. There is an overlap. The third is the overlap.

Leo: Is the highest density Orion the ones that first showed up to Stan; the three that showed up to Stan?

Stan: (*Cocks his head to his left, and then moves head back and forth.*) Mmm. They are working with Stan, but no.

Leo: What density are they...were they?

Stan: Fifth density. They are us.

Leo: That was my question. Thank you. Is one of the other groups... one of the other groups in Orion what we would call Reptilian?

Stan: There are Reptilian races, yes. There are many groups: Dracor, Reptilian...mmm...dragons...yes, they are...mmm...some are enlightened, but most are...have their own agenda. They control. They manipulate...what you call the Grey race. There are two different types of Grey race that you know. There are taller Grey race. There are smaller Grey race and some races in-between...different colors. All of which are involved with Starseed. Starseed is important in the fact that he is a...word... he is star born. He is star born. He is Starseed. He is becoming aware...he is becoming aware of his purpose. He is becoming aware of who he is, and we believe his transformation will happen soon. He will know where he is from. He is...mmm... *(deep breath)*...Orion...Orion...and Orions are warlike. Mmm... the system...mmm...the three systems are warlike. And...mmm... fifth-density, fourth-density Orions have become enlightened and are...agree to...word...reincarnate to a thicker density to help this third-dimensional reality to ascend. The human race is ascending. But they must do it on their own terms.

Leo: So are you saying that Stan's soul is Orion?

Stan: Yes. He does not know this yet and it is good if you do not tell him. He will figure it out for himself. Mini steps. Little steps. He is very important. He is important in this transition. More than anybody he is important in this transition. He has been chosen. He has agreed to this.

Leo: Are you yourself Orion that is speaking through Stan?

Stan: I am what you call "Elohim."

Leo: Elohim?

Elohim: Yes. Mmm...It is your words not ours. We do not call ourselves that but it is OK if you do...

Leo: Which density are you?

Elohim: We are fifth.

Leo: And do the Elohim work with different civilizations in particular?

Elohim: Yes. We work with the human race and with fourth-density Orions. We are the first with Stan. *(Moves head from side to side.)*

Leo: So, there was a time when Stan started receiving information from the one who is called Grandpa. Is Grandpa also Elohim?

Elohim: Mmm. Grandpa is...mmm...Orion, fourth-level Orion. We work with this fourth-density, fourth level Orion. It is easier for fourth-density to appear as three-density, third-density...mmm... third-dimensional being. They still have that ability but it is harder for us. We have met Stan before. In the beginning there were three of us. We disguise ourselves to not upset the balance. We disguise ourselves to not alert. The others that do not want this to happen. And yes there are others...mmm...Reptilian and Greys that...who are manipulating the human race to their benefit. But it will not continue.

Lazarus: So the Orions of the present-future, are these the authors of what we are calling the hybrid girls, the hybrid children?

Elohim: Fourth-density Orions and us. I must explain, so you understand. It is true that in the future the human race is manipulated by the Grey race so much that there is little human left in them. So you might as well not say *humans*. You might as well say *Grey race*.

After watching the playback of this conversation, it put the finishing touches on Lazarus's story to me about the Looking Glass Project. Everything around my abductions, my contact, and the threat of the Black Ops was finally making sense to me. All the secrets, all the deception, all the hidden answers were being flushed out by the Elohim. As remarkable as these conclusions were, what would happen next would amaze everyone.

It was at this point that the telephone in Lucie's bedroom began ringing. The Elohim lifted his head off of the chair and started looking around (with eyes still closed) as if trying to figure out where the noise was coming from.

Leo: The telephone. A message is coming through on the telephone.

Elohim: I see. *(Turns his head toward the direction of the ringing as if looking into the ceiling. He then holds his right hand up in the direction of the upstairs master bedroom as if saying, "Stop." The phone stopped ringing immediately.)*

Leo: *(Chuckles, amazed at what had just happened.)*

Elohim: *(Turns his head toward Lucie.)* I am sorry. I might have damaged your phone.

As Leo continued the questions, Lucie tiptoed out of the room and up the stairs to the master bedroom to examine the three cordless phones she had put away. A few minutes later she returned, mouthing the words, "They're gone."

Leo: Is the council that you are associated with part of what is called the Galactic Federation?

Elohim: Your words, but yes. There are different...what you call... federations. [The federation I belong to] is higher density. We are working with Stan, Starseed.

Leo: So is the council that you are associating with more closely described as what people call Celestials?

Elohim: Yes.

Leo: So you are part of the Celestial Council, then?

Elohim: Yes.

Leo: So is there an aspect of the Angelic Realm that is higher—

Elohim: (*Interrupting*) Yes, yes. They are higher. You call them Angelic, yes. They are a higher density.

Leo: Higher than the Elohim?

Elohim: Mmm. Yes, humans do not understand. Elohim [are of the] same [realm]. I cannot explain [in terms that humans can understand].

Leo then decided to take the questions in another area that had puzzled most of us. It was time to clear up all the mysteries.

Leo: One of the points we need cleared up is whether there have been any military or governmental abductions in the past?

Elohim: Yes.

Leo: How many?

Elohim: Two.

Leo: And this was to do what?

Elohim: Investigate. To experiment. They want information to misguide.

Leo: Was there any effort to intimidate or scare?

Elohim: Absolutely. But Starseed is higher than that.

Leo: Ah. What about his seeing the Insectoid or the Mantis People? Did that really happen?

Elohim: Yes. You must understand, there is agreement with some races and the government.

Leo: So are the Insectoids working with the military, the government?

Elohim: They are an old species. We are an old species. They are third- and fourth-density beings. There are multiple species involved with this.

Leo: So, are they working with the Orions?

Elohim: It is still unclear. Some are and some aren't. It is complicated. There is more to this than you can understand. They are on the fence.

Leo: So in the one abduction where Stan looks over and sees a small Grey, which I understand works with the Orions...

Elohim: Some do. Some do not.

Leo: And he saw a Mantis as well.

Elohim: Yes.

Leo: So was that one of the Mantises that was working with the Orions?

Elohim: They are on the fence. They do not yet know what to make of this situation. It was not military. It was a one-time abduction experience. Not an abduction...an introduction. Abduction is harsh.

Leo: Was that particular Mantis working with the Orions?

Elohim: No. Let me explain. There is a war. All know this. There are some that do not want this and there are some that do. There are some that are on the fence—both sides are trying to sway them to be on their side. Starseed was fearful because he had never seen anything like this. These are an old species, less spiritual than some but very intelligent. They do not [have] much compassion.

That's what the Possum Lady—an Elohim in disguise—was doing with the Mantis who had been witness to my abduction ("introduction"). The Elohim weren't looking for an ally in the war over Earth. They were looking for a way to bring peace to all civilizations. That's why the Possum Lady wanted the Mantis to see that I was far more advanced than the Mantis People thought. Ultimately, the Elohim wanted the Mantis People to see that humanity itself was far more advanced in ways the Mantis People had yet to realize. The Elohim were about to reveal the secret key not only to humanity but to all the Star Nations. That had to mean that the ancient and greatly respected Mantis People were essential in bringing an end to galactic war.

Leo: OK. We are told that some of the Greys that work with the Dracos do not have souls. Is this correct?

Elohim: That is correct. A soul is a human term. Energy changes, it does not go away. Do you understand?

Leo: I'd like to understand more with regard to the notion of souls.

Elohim: Souls are consciousness. [They are] an energy from the Oneness. You are familiar with Oversoul?

Leo: Yes.

Elohim: All are connected [via the] Oversoul. There is a subsoul and an Oversoul. There is a reality that everything is connected to a Oneness. Energy splits itself. It is still energy, but when energy passes, it continues. When the third-dimensional shell passes, the energy still continues. Do you understand?

Leo: I think so. But just to make sure, are you saying that even the Greys who do not have what we call souls are part of this?

Elohim: Everything is part of the Oneness. Some energy is stronger than others. That is all. Everything is connected. Everything has energy.

Leo: Can we get information on what is called the Audrey voice? Is the Audrey voice...

Elohim: *(Interrupting)* Children.

Leo: It's the children behind the Audrey voice?

Elohim: Yes.

Leo: How many of the children?

Elohim: Mainly, Kioma.

Leo: Kioma?

Elohim: There are two [sources]. Some are not of the children. Some are a deception. Stan understands this. And Lisa and Stan do not trust this. And that is fine.

Leo: Are any of the hybrid children the future woman who showed up when he was five years old?

Elohim: Kioma.

Leo: Okay. And does Kioma move between present and future?

Elohim: Yes. They were designed to move between third and fourth realities, and [between] time. Humans do not understand time.

Leo: I get that. So can Kioma show up as both an adult and a child?

Elohim: Again, humans do not understand time. She is human also. Humans [must grow], so she must grow. But she has the ability to traverse those densities. She is an adult in the future, but she can come back. Do you understand?

Leo: Yes.

Elohim: She is very smart.

Leo: I think we are getting that message.

Elohim: Blue eyes. Orions are not genetically born with blue eyes. They must become enlightened to obtain the blue eyes. Kioma and the children—there are some that do not have blue eyes. But Lisa's child is very smart.

Leo: Which one is Lisa's child?

Elohim: Unnamed.

Leo: OK. Whose child is Trilly?

Elohim: Trilly is Heidi's. She plays a role. She and Lisa's child [and] Kioma—they are friends—sisters. They play a major role.

Leo: Can you give us information about that major role?

Elohim: No.

Leo: Can you tell us what Lisa's role is with the nine hybrids that have been revealed?

Elohim: She is with Starseed. She supports Starseed. One of the nine is from part of Lisa and part of Starseed—as a scientific test, an experiment.

Leo: Like research?

Elohim: Research. We wanted to see. We wanted to create a multidimensional being. Do you understand?

Leo: Uh, how many of the nine are part of this experiment?

Elohim: All. One in particular.

Leo: Which one?

Elohim: A female child. Kioma.

Leo: Are any of the hybrids male?

Elohim: Yes.

Leo: How many?

Elohim: Three. They are less important. They are still important but the female is most important.

Leo: And what about the one who calls herself Trilly?

Elohim: Trilly. Yes. There are three in succession: Kioma, first; Trilly is third. The other one has no name yet.

Leo: Does that mean she just names herself?

Elohim: Yes. That is correct.

Leo: Will that information come forward later?

Elohim: If it is important. [There are nine children in all.] There were [three] more but they did not survive. They were from a woman before Victoria. [The woman] passed away [in a car accident]. The children did not survive [our] first tries, our first trials. Do you understand?

Leo: Can you tell us how Victoria came to be a part of the hybrid creations?

Elohim: She was pre-chosen just like Starseed was pre-chosen. Heidi and Lisa later were associated. [This was all part of] a test, [the research].

Leo: Can you tell us if these hybrids have what we call souls?

Elohim: Yes.

Leo: Are there other Greys that at one time were part human, like the P-45s?

Elohim: Humans are a conglomeration. Humans are mainly a conglomeration of Orion and Sirian. There are other things mixed in. There are multiple races. That is correct. There will be an extra race to help with the ascension...what you call the shift.

Leo: Then what can you tell us about these hybrid girls? Why are they here?

Elohim: They are important. They are important to the work that Starseed is doing. They are important to Starseed. They are of Starseed. They are of Orion and they are of us. There is a mix. There is a reason for this. The children have the ability to traverse both three-dimensional and four-dimensional...mmm... realities...and they are to help with the transition. They are the key. Starseed is the key. You are the key. Leo Sprinkle is the key; Lisa is the key. Others involved with Starseed are the key.

Not only were we learning that humans were hybrids themselves, but we also learned the true nature of these children. Unlike the other hybrids, who were created by ETs with less favorable agendas wanting to infiltrate, these hybrids were created to help raise consciousness, and more interestingly, the Elohim brought them here to foster a new race, a sixth race!

Modern anthropology states that there are five races:
1) Mongoloid (Asian and American Indian)
2) Caucasoid (European)
3) Australoid (Australian and Oceanic)
4) Negroid (East African Black)
5) Capoid (South African Black)

Each of the races has its own physical characteristics. If these children are indeed part of a sixth race, their most prominent characteristics will no doubt be their beautiful, oversized, slanted eyes! How would these children be accepted into a world with so many bigots, where wars are started over race and religion? It would be a daunting task for the Elohim, to be sure.

Leo: We are told that Stan's DNA may play a part. Is this true?

Elohim: Yes. And so does yours.

Leo: One of the things we are interested in is the role of DNA in this. The reason we are asking the question is that other sources have basically said that human DNA is what the Greys call "royal DNA." The Andromedans call human DNA "noble DNA" because it has the ability to connect all of the worlds.

Elohim: Yes. This is true.

Leo: And one of the aspects of DNA that humans have is also Angelic?

Elohim: That is true also. That is what you call Nephilim. Nephilim, if I'm not mistaken. Nephilim. Stan's words.

Leo: So there are aspects of human DNA that are Nephilim and Angelic? Is that what you are saying?

Elohim: There are multiple combinations. There are parts of many races involved with human DNA. Orion and Sirian and others. It is a spiritual agreement to do this. It has helped to raise the third-dimensional reality. Do you understand?

Leo: I do. Is this why the hybrid girls are not safe here? Are they being threatened?

Elohim: Yes. There are those that do not want the [agreement to be fulfilled]. There are those who have their own agenda. But they will not succeed.

Leo: Who are they?

Elohim: There are races that have controlled the human race, but the human race is greater than they know. They will understand soon. Unfortunately, there are those who will be left behind. This is where Starseed comes in. This is where Starseed has been placed to help. [Ascension] is for everybody, including Zeta Reticuli Greys...even what you call the Reptilian race—Dracos. It is to help raise the vibration of all. The human race has been designed to raise the vibration of the third-dimensional density and all that are involved with it. The human race has been designed to become enlightened by love and compassion and understanding. All are equally connected. That includes compassion for the Grey races—but humans do not have to put up with what some of them are doing, put up with their agenda. Some Greys are of a weak genetic makeup, and Stan is driven to want to help everybody, including them, but he must understand it is not his responsibility. He will learn this. He is eager to help everyone. This is part of his makeup, but he must focus on enlightening.

Leo: We are already getting information from geneticists that this [genetic change] is occurring.

Elohim: Yes. It is. It started on January 11th of 1992. The gate was activated, an Orion gate at the center of Orion: Alnitak, Alnilam, and Mintaka. The stargate is near the center star of Alnilam. The Orion gate is the 11-11 gate. That is why Starseed sees 11-11. He is a major part of that higher-density rising of vibration. That is the significance of 11-11. The 11-11 gate has been activated. *(He looks over at Lazarus.)* You were a part of that. Egypt. *(Lazarus lowers his eyes.)* It was activated in Egypt when you were there different times and helped. The star gate was not open all the way. You helped open it further. Do you understand?

Leo: Are there other hybrid races that are also going to be a part of the Earth, other than the Orions?

Elohim: Yes. There are some that are here now. There are multiple [races]. This is not just for the human race; this is for multiple races. There is a connection. There is a Oneness. We hope that this will affect multiple races at multiple levels. There are multiple levels of races that are more advanced, mentally. And they have forgotten their place. Their genetic makeup has become weak because of this. A melding of the technological and spiritual will make for a much stronger human race.

Leo: Are there hybrids that have been created by the Greys who are living with the Dracos?

Elohim: Oh. Yes.

Leo: And what was their purpose?

Elohim: To infiltrate. You must understand not all of what you call the Grey race is [deceptive]. There are some, including some Dracos, that are working toward a higher vibration. There are some that are not. There is, as Starseed says, a war—even between government and off-world entities. There are those fighting for [ascension] to happen. It must happen for all...it must happen for all to benefit. Not just the human race.

Leo: Thank you for that. There is information we have that there are two other sets of hybrids: one that comes from Andromeda and one that comes from the Tau Ceti, who are green in color. Is this information accurate?

Elohim: There are multiple hybrids. There are multiple civilizations and various star systems. There are multiple connections with the human race. All are important.

Leo: Is there anything more we should know about the role of the hybrids?

Elohim: They are important. They are important to the work that Starseed is doing. They are of Starseed. They are of Orion and they are of us. There is a mix. There is a reason for this. The children have the ability to traverse both third-dimensional and fourth-dimensional realities. They are to help with the transition.

Lazarus: Is Stan working with any of the Celestials?

Elohim: Yes. Celestials...A human word.

Leo: Angels?

Elohim: Yes. (*Pause*) Elohim.

Lazarus: Can you address any information about what is called First Contact, which came through in the predictions?

Elohim: It will happen. But it is up to humanity. It must be on their terms, or enlightenment—the raising of the vibration—will not happen. Support Stan. The book is important. You were guided.

When the session ended, I was briefed about what had been said in regression.

After finally calming down, I looked up to see everyone else looking at me. Lucie, as usual, put everything in perspective. "If I can't find my three remote phones, I'm sending you a bill. It's bad enough when you come over here that you blow out half the light bulbs."

Everyone laughed at this burst of light-heartedness. It somehow grounded us again.

After searching the entirety of the house, we finally discovered the three handsets—lined up neatly on the bed in the third bedroom, clear across the house from where she had placed the phones in the first place.

Lucie picked up the phones and tested them to make sure that traveling through three walls hadn't damaged them.

"They work," she reported. "You're lucky, Stan. Your seraph friend's little trick about got your ass kicked!" she said. It was another light-hearted Lucie quip, but you could tell in her eyes that she was overwhelmed by the sheer magnitude of what had happened.

Looking around, I saw everyone had a glazed look. It's hard to stay away from a sense of awe in the face of the mystery of the universe as it unfolds right before your eyes.

"As soon as you get back from your trip, Stan, we really need to discuss what we have learned here today," Lazarus told me.

In the week that followed, I was busy getting ready for my next conference in Aztec, New Mexico. This conference was the biggest event of my life, and not because of the size or location, or even the other speakers who were attending. Instead, very special visitors, the likes of which I had never met, had vowed to try to attend.

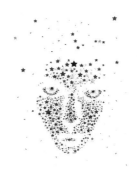

Chapter Twenty-One

The Aztec Conference

Aztec, New Mexico
March 2010

Many years after the 1948 UFO crash near Aztec, New Mexico, the folks at the Aztec Public Library created an annual conference to commemorate the event and help fund the local library system. I was invited to speak there in 2010.

As was the case with all my speaking engagements, Victoria had expressed an interest in joining us. Over the few years that we got to know her, she had become an avid supporter and loved to go with us on our speaking adventures. Unfortunately, this time Victoria was unable to get the time off work.

While Victoria and I were discussing the disappointing news over the phone, our conversation was interrupted when we noticed a loud click on the line.

"Daddy? Daddy? Can you hear me?" a little girl's voice interjected.

"Stan! Get your digital recorder," Victoria ordered. "Hurry! It's one of the girls."

"Hold on, I've got one in my desk."

I set the phone down and dashed to my desk. After rummaging through the drawer, I found it, turned it on, and reached for the phone again.

"Stan, do you have it? Do you have it?" Victoria asked.

"Yes," I yelled back. "It's on."

"Is this Kioma?" Victoria asked tenderly.

"Yes..." responded the childlike voice.

"Ohhh, sweet girl, we can hear you," Victoria cooed.

"Is somebody playing a joke on us?" I asked.

"You're silly," was the playful response.

"Silly? Why am I silly? OK, if this is who I think it is, then when are we going to see you again?"

"That's why we're calling. We might be able to see you at your next talk."

"In Aztec?" asked Victoria.

"I've got to go. Bye."

"Oh my God!" gasped Victoria.

"Are you still there?" I asked.

There was no response.

"This is amazing," continued Victoria.

We chatted about the possibility of actually meeting the children. After playing our recordings again over the phone to each other, Victoria challenged me to find them at the conference. A pleasant trip to a library-sponsored event that publicly celebrated a long-forgotten UFO crash now took on the prospect of a dramatic encounter. We decided to let close friends know of the phone call.

Among those close to us is Paola Harris, who, as it turned out, had also received an invitation to speak—a significant addition to this small-town event. A well-known Italian journalist, Paola is a spunky, outspoken, ash-blonde spitfire who's interested in nothing less than reporting Earth-shattering contact cases, which has made her one of the leading researchers in the Exopolitics movement. Her contact with the Vatican was instrumental in the Vatican's coming forward about life on other worlds.

The conference sponsors had a limited budget, which meant we had to find a way to cut costs on our end. I checked to see if our good friend Lucie might be going to the conference also. Since Paola lived fairly close, I suggested that we all share the ride and drive down to New Mexico together.

By the time we got into Durango, Colorado, the weather had turned really nice for a late March day. The scenery between Denver and Pueblo is like a journey into different worlds. The choke of traffic in Denver yields to the pines of Colorado Springs. The road edges along a mesa as you approach Aztec, with the drop-off on the passenger side revealing immense and breathtaking low lands of Pinion pine and Yucca cactus.

Since the speaker's dinner was scheduled for 6 p.m., we had little time to unload the SUV, clean up, and meet the conference organizer at a local bar. Katie, the organizer, was just as charming as the town, and her bubbly welcome made us all feel like celebrities.

Aztec reminded me of the type of town you see in Western movies, and I almost expected a gunslinger to bust through the door for an old-fashioned game of poker during our dinner. Meeting the other speakers turned out to be both interesting and informative, especially when I discovered that the conference was to be held in the local Masonic Lodge. My eyes widened at the news, as I'd always been curious about the rituals of Freemasonry. The next day I stared in disbelief at how large the lodge stood in a tiny town of 7,000.

Paola, Lisa, Lucie and I spent Friday morning setting up our vendor spaces with books and CDs.

"Do you think they will show up?" Paola whispered.

We knew exactly who she was talking about. It was on all our minds. Curious about the possibility of meeting them in a Freemason's lodge, I began to check out the building. There were three sets of doors to the lodge. The front double doors opened to a lobby where attendees registered for the conference. To the right of the lobby, a hallway led to the vendor room. Our table allowed us a good view of anyone entering the building. The lobby branched into the main auditorium where, to the left, a single door opened to the outside. A hefty rock propped the door open to create ventilation during the presentations. The third door was back in the far right corner, blocked shut by conference staff tables and camera people. If my hybrid children were going to show up, it seemed the only safe way to sneak in was through the side door, but that didn't seem possible because the entire auditorium would be filled with people. I even went so far as to check the upper levels for balconies but found none.

Paola noticed my scoping out the building. "Don't worry, Stan. The rest of us will be looking, too."

The conference started late Friday with two speakers taking up the rest of the day. I had a hard time concentrating on what the speakers were saying, or what book buyers were asking me. I had been watching carefully how the conference organizers monitored the crowd, wondering if the girls would try to sneak in. It seemed that the unusual looking children might catch the attention of others. As badges were being issued, I noticed that other than a small side door, which was only open during a break or a transition between speakers, there was really no other way in than through the front door. Baffled by how they might otherwise sneak in, I gave up hope of seeing them here, despite the promise on the telephone.

By Saturday morning I was plagued with a creeping sense of disappointment; the possibility of meeting the children was becoming more unlikely. Since Paola and I were the last two speakers of the event, we spent the morning searching for them. Meanwhile, Lisa took care of the business of selling our books at our vendor table. Failing to notice any children in the crowd, I finally gave up and went back to where Lisa was.

"How are sales going?" I asked.

"We're almost sold out of books. Who would've thought that 250 people would show up for a conference like this in such a small town? I guess we can have you sign CDs of your music if we run out books. This place is crammed."

I decided Lisa should have a break. "I know you'd like to hear some of the speakers. Why don't you mosey into the hall and catch some of the talks."

"Well, OK," she said, as she slipped into the darkness of the full auditorium.

When Lisa returned, she started talking about license plates, which meant she had gone to the parking lot for a smoke.

"There's a bunch from Roswell," she said. "I saw 'I Believe' on one with a flying saucer on the license plate cover. Another bumper sticker said, 'Wear your seatbelt. It makes it harder for UFOs to suck you out of your car.' But my favorite was, 'UFOs are real. The government's fake.' There are people from as far away as Kansas and Oklahoma here."

The last speaker of the morning finally finished. From the attached kitchen, volunteers brought us cold ham and cheese sandwiches and a bag of chips. I was so hungry I would have eaten paper. Most went outside into the parking lot to enjoy their meal, but I stayed in the vendor room to guard the table. I also started to feel as if I had the flu. On the drive down, Paola had complained that she was just recovering from being sick, but seeing that she was getting better, we didn't give it a second thought. Unfortunately whatever Paola had come down with, it looked like I might suffer the same fate.

After lunch, I continued my watch, pacing the building. The packed place did not present the right conditions for the girls to show up. Nor did I see any sign of Black Ops agents (dressed up as Average Joes) who would normally monitor what I talk about at lectures. Lisa had suspicions of a few who seemed to be trying to get information from people, asking a lot of questions but buying nothing.

I made one last circle of the building before leaving to get ready for my part of the conference. Lucie returned from her visit to McDonald's, ice cream in hand. Paola had begun her talk.

By then Lucie also started to feel sick, so I escorted her to the motel since I had to get back to change my clothes anyhow. I kept glancing around as we left, but by now it was obvious that the girls weren't going to show.

Eventually I returned to the motel room to change clothes and get my equipment. As I dressed, I mused at the depth of my own disappointment. I tried to snap myself out of my low mood by mulling over what I would say during my presentation. With so much disinformation flooding our world, and so much negativity from our own media, I found myself taking my role as messenger very seriously. Fortunately, by the time I drove back to the Masonic Lodge parking lot, my thoughts were entirely focused on my talk.

With laptop in hand, I opened the door of the SUV to step out. As I fumbled to collect all my stuff, I dropped my computer and case on the ground. Just as I was picking things up, I was startled by the presence of a little girl standing there. Looking up, I could see she was holding a single-stalked cluster of yellow chrysanthemums in her hand. Being bent over I had a hard time seeing her face. Since there were no children at all at the conference, I was bewildered by this small child. For an instant I got a glimpse of her blondish hair, gathered in pigtail fashion. There was something familiar about her, but I did not remember seeing her before.

She was still holding out the flowers to give to me when I heard a sweet, melodic voice, bubbly with innocence, say "This is for you."

"Thank you," I said as I reached out to accept the gift. I once again fumbled and almost dropped my computer as I quickly scanned the parking lot and the front of the building for the girl's parents. I wanted to thank them with a courtesy nod, and also thank them for allowing their daughter to approach me with the gift. But there were no adults in sight. *What parent would allow their four- or five-year-old child to be alone in a parking lot, let alone give a stranger a gift?* I wondered. Then I heard her coo, "I love you."

In the few seconds it took for me to look up and respond, she was gone. *What the hell! Where did she go?* All of a sudden it hit

Photo of me taken by our friend Paola Harris a few hours after these flowers where given to me by my hybrid daughter.

me—it was one of the hybrid girls. Her voice was similar to one of the children who had spoken on the phone. As I brushed off my laptop, I knew I had to get to my talk, but I also knew I had to look for her.

After searching around the building, I entered the lodge and went straight to Lisa, still clutching the stem of yellow flowers. I began telling her what had happened.

"Did anyone else see her?" Lisa asked.

My frustration flared. Her lack of enthusiasm seemed to indicate she didn't believe me.

"Do you think I'm making this up?"

"No, Stan, I'm simply asking if anyone else saw her," she snapped. "It would be a good idea to ask around, don't you think?"

"I haven't had time to ask anyone," I snapped back. Shuffling away from Lisa, I went to get a bottle of water and started asking people who were gathered at the refreshment counter at back of the room if anyone had seen a little girl with blonde pigtails. There didn't seem to be anyone.

As I re-entered the vendor area where Lisa sat waiting for my return, I noticed her beckoning me to quickly come to her. "Stan, is that the little girl you saw?" she asked excitedly.

"No, I told you she had pigtails."

"There is something odd about her; I can feel it."

There, in the back section, sat a young girl with long stringy blonde hair. I tried to see what Lisa was so worked up about, but in the dim lighting of the auditorium I could see nothing out of the ordinary regarding the child. From my vantage point she looked like any other little girl.

"You should take a picture of her," Lisa told me. "You can't see her like I did because she sat down where it's dark."

Shuffling several feet closer to the girl, I made sure I had the girl in the view screen of the camera. I was nervous about disrupting Paola's talk. But to appease my wife, I took the picture of the girl in the very back row of the room, making sure to stay back far enough not to blind everyone in the audience.

The girl suddenly got up and walked toward the front of the room. I went back and handed the camera to Lisa, and then started gathering my presentation materials, all the while clutching the stem of yellow flowers in my hand. Not giving the girl in the back row a second thought, my mind went back over the perplexing events that had transpired in the parking lot.

At that same moment, a woman by the name of Linda sat equally perplexed in her seat among the crowd. She was distracted by the presence of a young girl to her right, who seemed to be looking for someone or something. Linda's entire focus had now shifted away from Paola's question and answer period to the little girl who looked to be eight or nine years old. She was wandering around the front of the room. Linda sat stunned—she had never seen such huge, beautiful eyes. They were so blue that they were almost violet. *I wonder if she needs help,* Linda thought to herself. *I would help you if I could.*

Linda's heart started pounding frantically when the little girl looked straight at her and started walking in her direction. *Oh, my god,* Linda thought, *it's as if she's read my mind!* With the shyness of a lost child, the four-foot girl scooted into the empty seat next to Linda. An essence of magic and wonder surrounded the child. She turned her head and looked into Linda's eyes.

"I can't find my dad."

Linda tried to comfort her. "He can't be far away. What does he look like?"

There was no answer.

As Linda waited for the child to answer, she noticed that the clothing on the child was almost as unusual as her eyes. She wore a greyish sweatsuit made of a shiny material and a diamond-shaped pendant that sparkled wildly in the dimly lit room. It was as if it had a hundred tiny LED lights flickering on and off all over it. The pendant was framed by her blonde hair that hung in strings over her shoulder.

"May I ask a favor of you?" asked the child.

"Of course, dear. What is it?"

"Will you give my dad a message?"

Although puzzled by the unusual request, Linda dove into her purse to search for a pen and paper. All she could find was an old receipt. She smoothed the wrinkles from the paper.

"OK, what would you like me to tell your dad?"

The girl began firing information faster than Linda could write it down. As she struggled to accurately transcribe the message, the child suddenly got up and walked away. Linda scribbled the rest of the message while at the same time trying to keep an eye on the unusual girl. She watched as the little girl walked to the side door toward the back of the auditorium and slipped out.

As I made my way up to the podium, the freshly acquired flower in hand, I knew that I had to begin my presentation with the story of the hybrid children.

"Hello, everyone. I usually start my presentation out with my first UFO sighting and work my way to the present day. But today, I am skipping forward a bit and will work my way backward, because something incredible just happened to me in the parking lot. Sorry, I am really shaky." As I relayed the entire story, I lifted up the flower I had received. "If anyone has seen the little girl I just described, I'd really like for you to come talk to me after the presentation." I then proceeded to play the phone call that Victoria and I had recently gotten from the girls.

Looking toward the back of the room, I saw Lisa and Paola positioning themselves like guards.

"Paola," Lisa whispered, "they're here."

"Who's here?" Paola asked, searching the room.

"The girls are here, two of them. Stan saw one of the girls in the parking lot and I think we just got a picture of a second girl, sitting in the back of the room. Of course, Stan thinks she is just a normal kid. I don't agree."

"Are you serious? Why did they come while I was talking? Where are they? I have to see them." Paola was on her feet, dragging Lisa to the vendor room. "Show me the picture."

Lisa fumbled with the camera, all the while telling Paola about the beautiful girl with the amazing eyes and high slanting eyebrow bones. As the picture of the beautiful girl appeared, Paola gasped, "That's amazing. Zoom it in. Zoom it! Look at that necklace, how pretty. I need to get a closer look at those eyes."

"I can't get the darn thing to zoom in," confessed Lisa. "I don't know how to do it. I'll have to get Stan to fix it. We'll have to wait until he's done talking."

"Maybe they'll come back," said Paola. "Let's get back to our spot where we can see all of the doors."

About forty minutes later, Paola grabbed Lisa's hand. "Look at the side door."

Lisa noticed a young man sneaking in through the side door of the auditorium. He made his way straight toward them, stopping about fifteen feet away.

"That boy is not normal," Paola insisted, nearly chewing on Lisa's ear. "He's bigger than a basketball center. He's got to be close to eight feet tall."

The two women giggled, drawing the attention of those around them and eliciting a shush or two.

"How can a boy of maybe thirteen be so tall?" Lisa asked.

Not to be dissuaded by the hushes, Lisa and Paola continued to whisper as they kept tabs on the boy.

"Project a thought at him," instructed Paola.

Intently, Lisa focused her thoughts and sent them in the direction of the tall boy: "If you can understand me, I want you to know that if you were around at my house, you could reach all the things I have trouble even seeing." Lisa froze as the young man's head slowly turned and looked directly into her eyes. He simply smiled and nodded. "Whoa! It worked! Did you see that?"

"Yes. What incredible blue eyes," Paola pronounced to another round of shushing.

A great smile again spread across his thin face.

"Oh, my gosh," Lisa whispered.

"It worked, it worked," Paola whispered back. "Do it again. Do it again. It worked."

Lisa giggled, "He's going to think we are crazy ol' bats putting the moves on him. I'll be right back; keep an eye on him." Lisa had decided to go to the registration table near the entrance to check with Katie. "Do you know anything about that really tall kid who just came in the side door?" she asked.

Katie did not recognize him. After easing up to him, Katie introduced herself, chatted for a few seconds, and returned to Lisa. Katie leaned into Lisa. "He's not going to stay," she said. "He's just here for a few minutes. Did you see his eyes...?"

That was what Lisa wanted to hear. She was now sure this had to be another hybrid.

She then noticed the tall young man suddenly bolting out of the side door. Oddly it was just seconds before two burly military-looking figures came bursting in through the front doors and all while I was still speaking. Katie intercepted them.

"What the hell is going on here?" asked one of the men loudly. "Can we come in or what?"

"Our last speaker is talking," said Katie, "We're about ready to end the conference, but you are welcome to look around."

Lisa whispered five words into Paola's ear: "Black Ops just walked in."

Both men stood around six-foot tall and sported military crew cuts. The two thugs muscled their way to the vendor's room, rudely rifling their way through the materials on the display tables. As they shambled along like two bulls, they constantly scanned the vendor's room, the hallway, and the auditorium.

One of the only vendors in the room at the time welcomed them. "Can I help you guys?"

They glared at him as if he had insulted them.

Finding nothing to satisfy their search, they headed for the front door. As they approached Katie they nodded their heads in my direction and hissed, "That guy's scarier than Obama."

"Well, I guess we all can't be Republicans, now can we?" retorted Katie. One of the men suddenly spun around, moving quickly toward the table where Katie stood. Undisguised hatred flashed in his eyes as he rushed at her with a fist in the air. Katie flattened herself against the wall out of his reach. The two men quickly left.

Even with all the commotion my talk went off without a hitch. After the question-and-answer period, I went to our vendor table to sign books and talk with guests.

"Stan, I have to talk to you," Lisa demanded. "One of the boys was here too. Stan? Are you listening to me, damn it...this is important." There were so many people that I couldn't listen to Lisa and talk to them at the same time. I could tell she was angry for being ignored, but this was important. I needed to see if anyone had seen the girl with the pigtails. I was surprised by the number of witnesses telling me their stories about seeing the girl. A husband and wife had seen the pigtailed girl in the Safeway grocery store all by herself. They thought it very strange that she would be wandering the store alone. A few people had seen a girl walking in the hall wearing a grey sweatsuit. But what really drew one witness's attention was the shape of her large blue eyes. He said it was more than that; it was the amount of love that could be felt coming from them. Two others had noticed a marvelous necklace the girl wore that blinked with a kind of light. [See photo on opposite page]

I was confused. I didn't remember a necklace on the girl in the parking lot. And some people saw a girl without pigtails. As I sat there trying to understand what everyone was saying all at the same time, I felt a tug on my arm.

"Hi, Stan. My name is Linda, and I have something to tell you," she said with breathless anticipation. "Come with me, please. It is very important." She gave me little choice as she began dragging me into a corner of the room, as far away from other people as possible. Lisa stood directly in front of us, concealing us as we sat in the corner chairs behind our vendor table. "I talked with one of the little girls," she said. "She asked me to give you a message."

"What? Are you serious?"

She unfolded the crumpled paper on which she had taken notes.

"It wasn't until I heard your presentation that any of this made any sense to me. I almost flipped out when you started talking about the hybrid girls and how they have been communicating with you.

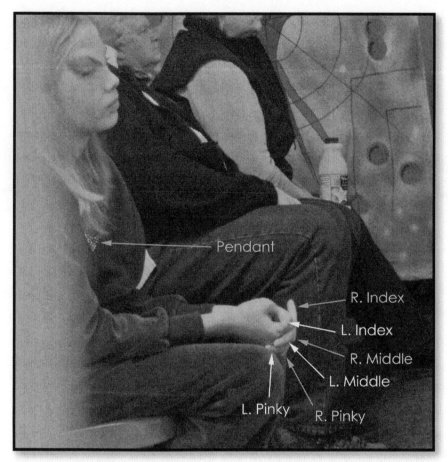

After researchers scrutinized this picture of who I believe is my hybrid daughter Suri, they realized she only had three fingers on each hand. You can also see the necklace everyone saw her wearing at the conference.

When you played their recordings, my heart nearly jumped out of my chest. The recorded voice reminded me of the voice of the girl who sat next to me. Her message was such a mystery to me. I almost threw it away. My heart was pounding when I realized that the girl who sat next to me was one of your girls, and she was asking me to give this message to you."

"What did she say?" I asked excitedly.

"She said she couldn't find her dad and asked me if I would do her a favor and leave her dad a message. I thought it was strange to leave a message for her dad with a total stranger and not give me his name or even a description of what he looked like. All I had in my purse to write on was an old receipt. She said, 'Tell Lisa my name is Suree or Siree. And tell Dad one boy's name is Nadu or Ndu.' She was talking so fast I had a hard time keeping up. She said, 'Tell daddy that we are here! We are here to help Earth. We are living on Unack or Unch'? It was hard for me to understand some of the words, so I wrote them like they sounded. When I asked her who her daddy was, she suddenly got up and left out the side door."

Stunned by Linda's story and the message, I felt a surge of excitement. I couldn't wait to get out of the room, away from all of the people so I could tell Lisa what had happened, and to take a closer look at the picture she had insisted I take. It suddenly all made sense. There were two girls who had come to visit. Little did I know that Lisa had interesting news for me as well. Not only about seeing the boy, but about the Black Ops visit as well. Amazingly, this was the first time that the general public had been involved in what had been, up to this time, only my and Lisa's personal encounters.

As if Katie had heard my thoughts, she announced that everyone had to immediately leave the building. We were all late for a private dinner party that had been set up for the speakers.

I wanted to talk to both girls, to engage them in a conversation, to let them know how much I cared about them. I also wanted to tell them how much I appreciated that they had put their lives at risk to visit me.

I asked Linda if she would write an affidavit witness report for me. A few days later, she sent Lisa this email.

Subject: Aztec New Mexico message from the little girl
Date: Tuesday, March 30, 2010, 12:42 PM, March 29, 2010

Hello Lisa,

My name is Linda W---; I am the woman at the Aztec UFO Conference that got the message from the little girl. I have a friend that has talked to you on Facebook before. She found your email address for me. I was hoping that you could get this to your husband. I lost his business card. As I promised him, here is my witnesses report. I was definitely shaken up by the experience!

March 27, 2010, I was attending the Aztec UFO Conference in Aztec New Mexico. I was listening to Paola Harris speak when I first noticed a little girl walking towards the front of the room looking for someone. My god, her eyes were something else! I would have never believed it if I didn't see it for myself. As if she heard my thoughts she stopped and sat down right next to me. I remember that she was wearing a grey outfit and had stringy blond hair. I thought she was part oriental but it was something more; her eyes were just too big!

She said she couldn't find her dad and asked me if I would do her a favor and leave her dad a message. All I had in my purse to write on was an old receipt. If I am not mistaken I think she said 'Tell Lisa my name is Suree or Siree and tell dad one boy's name is Nadu or Ndu'?

She was talking so fast I had a hard time keeping up. She told me to 'tell her daddy that we are here! We are here to help Earth. We are living on Unack or Unch'? I didn't understand what she said. When I asked her who here daddy was she suddenly got up and left out the side door. It wasn't until Stan's talk that I knew who the message was for. Tell Stan I hope this is what he wanted.

Sincerely
Linda W---

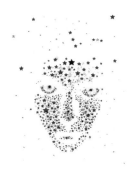

Chapter Twenty-Two

A Last Encounter at the Stanley Hotel

April 2011

"Have you recovered yet?" Lazarus asked with a chuckle.

"Barely," I replied, knowing full well Lazarus was not calling for a social visit.

"Well, Stan," he said, "if you have time I would like to meet up with you one last time to say my goodbyes."

"Goodbye?" I said surprised. "What do you mean 'goodbye'?"

"Well...I have completed what I set out to do, and it is now time for me to move on. If you meet with me, we can talk about things over lunch."

If nothing else Lazarus loved making a statement, and as we were trying to decide where to meet he suggested the Stanley Hotel in Estes Park, Colorado.

There was no better place to make a statement than the grand Stanley Hotel, I thought to myself.

The remote mountain destination seemed a good place to talk about deep metaphysical issues at leisure, and considering it's been rated the most haunted hotel in the United States by many a paranormal group and the Sci Fi Channel, what better place to talk about the paranormal? Considering the irony of it all, I knew that was why Lazarus chose it. And after thinking about it, I actually did need a change of scenery from the hustle and bustle of city life.

Later, driving up the mountain pass, I couldn't help but reflect on how we had picked the perfect location to meet for a day-long discussion. We were driving on the very road that was taken by architect Freelan O. Stanley in 1903. My van, with the V-6 engine, struggled up the winding 7,500-foot climb. I thought about Stanley driving on this road in his own invention—the Stanley Steamer automobile. In his day, the roads were unpaved and the entire landscape was unspoiled by commercialism. It was hard to imagine that these lands were even more serene and beautiful at one point.

Estes Park shimmered into view as I broke the crest of the mountainous climb. The Stanley Hotel sat on its perch, barely visible off in the distance. Its white, four-story exterior and red tile roof reflected the afternoon sunlight.

The Stanley Hotel in Estes Park, Colorado.

For a brief moment, I gazed at the beautiful mountains that surround the majestic hotel and felt connected to my destiny, whatever exactly that may be. *If this was real, and I'd come to believe it was, benevolent beings had chosen me among very few others. Of all people they had selected me to help spread a message that would benefit all humankind. If this was real, what's a guy like me supposed to say to that? And if I've somehow chosen this fate as well, like what the Elohim and what Grandpa have said, what does that say about a greater cosmic awareness? Are we indeed spiritual beings merely having a human experience?*

Questions continued to stir in the back of my mind as I reached the hotel and found a parking spot. Approaching the massive stairway leading to the main lobby, I thought about how Stephen King got his idea for *The Shining* after staying in the infamous room 217. I thought about how Jim Carrey had stayed in the very same room and left suddenly during the night. These days, though, stories such as these don't irk me as much as they used to.

As I climbed the last of the stairs and crossed the expansive porch, I thrust open the wooden doors. The hotel's interior beauty never failed to entrance me—the light green and cream-colored wallpaper, the polished wooden floors, the massive wooden fireplaces reminiscent of old Georgian architecture.

When I scanned the huge lobby, I spied Lazarus sitting in one of the dark brown leather chairs that flanked the fireplace at the west end. He waved his spindly hand as if he were in a parade. After greeting each other, we moved over to the bar, ordered some refreshments, and got down to business.

"Watching the video of my regression, I saw that the Elohim used my hand to make an unzipping motion," I began. "As I watched this, a light went on in my head—the Elohim were trying to tell me that they had visited me in what I thought was a dream. What I had thought to be a Grey appeared to me and started unzipping its skin. As the skin fell away, a bright whitish-blue being emerged and said to me, in the dream, 'We are Elohim.' The dream had haunted me for days. It now makes sense that the Elohim wanted me to understand that they have disguised themselves not only to me, but also to other races as they enter into Earth's history once again, this time to reveal 'the secret key.'"

"That's an interesting insight. I, too, had one based on your sessions," replied Lazarus. "This one revises the timeline story I was telling you. The Elohim said that those in the project had been deceived by the Greys, who had wanted the Secret Government to believe that Greys themselves came from humans. It was their attempt to keep the Secret Government in their good graces while deceptively pursuing their plot to replace humanity with Grey hybrids during the catastrophes of Timeline One—the same catastrophes the Possum Lady, who we now know was Elohim in disguise, had tried to warn you about."

"That's a pretty huge insight," I said.

Lazarus elaborated further. "Those on the Looking Glass Project had been deceived. The information from the Looking Glasses depends on the awareness of the person using the Looking Glass. So information from the Looking Glasses can be clouded if the awareness of the individual is clouded. Greys had fed distorted information to the Looking Glass Project people—they claimed they had come from humans, when in actuality they were only slightly human. Instead, the Timeline One scenario that actually would have taken place would have had most of humanity replaced by Grey hybrids. That DNA manipulation would later be the downfall of the Grey race because the DNA they had manipulated is leading to their own extinction."

"What I really got out of these sessions, Lazarus," I said with raised eyebrows, "is that everything around my abductions, my contact, and the threat of the Black Ops is finally making sense to me. All the secrets, all the deception, all the hidden answers were being fleshed out by the Elohim."

"The Elohim are as compassionate about the Greys as they are with all other species," noted Lazarus. "I wonder how compassionate humanity will be once it finds out the history of some of the Greys and other races who have done so much damage to humanity. What's becoming apparent is that the Elohim expect us not only to become compassionate people ourselves, but also to teach this compassion to the rest of our planet."

"I think that the transition, the shift, will happen naturally," I said. "Once the human race understands that they are not alone, it will change everything. And the vibration will be raised instantaneously. And that dormant coding that lies within human DNA will switch on. A plot eons in the making is about to unfurl throughout the third dimension. A great secret has been hidden within humanity since its beginnings, put there by the Angelic Realm and the Elohim. The secret key was hidden in humanity's DNA all along. What we found out from the Elohim was that humans are the only race in the universe other than the angels that carries, within it, angelic DNA. Only recently have other worlds of the star nations come to find this out. And only recently has humanity turned around its own near-extinction at the hands of the Greys and the Dracos by moving Earth into the consciousness of Oneness, thereby bringing forth Timeline Three. As tempting as it is to blame the Greys for everything, the truth of the matter is that they could not have done anything if we hadn't allowed it. And we did allow it. Parts of humanity made a bargain with them in the name of greed and control of the planet. What those humans didn't realize was that the Greys and the Dracos had studied us greatly. And what they almost pulled off, by appealing to our weaker side, our selfish side, our unchallenged arrogance, was having us embrace our own self-destruction. But because the few, who saw the inherent greatness within, rallied us to the call of compassion, and love, and Oneness, the veils of forgetfulness are now falling away. And what more and more of us are finally seeing is the inherent wonder that lies hidden within our own DNA."

Lazarus nodded. "Well spoken. In several appearances by the Angelic Realm, they have plainly stated, 'Our kind wish is to bind with your kind.' Only now do we realize what that means in the message from the Elohim. Not only are we the only race to carry angelic DNA, other than the angels themselves, we also are the only race capable of co-creating quantum realities without technology. It rests inherently within us. Like the ancient stories in the Bhagavad Gita say, 'I am the destroyer of worlds,' and 'I am the maker of new ones.'

"And the divine seeding of the cosmos will be borne by the coming hybrids," he added. "Kioma, Trilly, Suri, Nadu and the rest of the children are the harbingers of worlds to come. They stand as a great triumph of creation at the hands of the Elohim, the Priestly Orions, and humanity. They are the embodiment of the secret key— how humanity, considered so lowly by advanced civilizations, is the DNA chariot that leads all in the third dimensional worlds back to the Creator. In the Book of Psalms, 118:22, we find the perfect metaphor for this: 'The stone that the builders have rejected has become the cornerstone.'"

Lazarus smiled as he continued. "As we enter the shift, we, indeed, are leaving behind a world of war and strife and entering into a new world that brings forth new creation. And from this, we will usher forth undreamt changes among all the star nations. It's going to be a tough ride, but I believe we are becoming a new people, a people of divine destiny."

I laughed as another thought came to me. "I fell outta my seat when I heard the revelation about the Possum People. All of a sudden, the mystery around the Possum People became clear to me: There were no Possum People; they were Elohim in disguise. Had they been trying to move me into a grand plot on behalf of humanity, as well as maneuver the Mantis People into their grand scheme?"

"Speaking of the Elohim," said Lazarus, "I've done quite a bit of research on them from ancient histories."

I leaned forward. "I'm listening."

Lazarus smiled. "The Elohim are the ones responsible for creating humanity. The Bene Elohim, who they also had created, had walked the Earth creating havoc, leaving in charge their offspring, the Nephilim. It was the Nephilim who had enslaved humanity for eons through the royal lineages, acting as their minions. It was the Nephilim who altered our genetic code to dumb us down, leaving us with what scientists have thought to be 'junk' DNA. At first blush, one might be tempted to think the Elohim had screwed up and failed in their desire to create an incomparable race through humanity—but the Elohim were about to play their trump card on the universe itself.

"It's starting to make sense why Grandpa the Orion, in previous sessions you've shared with me, had so mysteriously answered the question about whether humanity was more advanced spiritually than his highly advanced race."

"Yes, I remember," I jumped in. "He had said, 'We are studying this.' And when asked about human origins, he had referred to a civilization far advanced from the Orions: 'As advanced as we are from you, they are as advanced from us. Humans are a conglomerate of races. There are offshoots that do not belong with humans, but in the struggle to find their origins, humans have accepted that they are from this particular species, apes. In fact, humans are a conglomeration of off-world and on-world races. You are much older than you think. You existed when what you call cave men existed, but in smaller groups, in little pockets.' I now know who Grandpa was talking about when he had referenced a race far in advance of his own. He was talking about the Elohim. Though terrible events and even more terrible treatment nearly destroyed humanity, we somehow prevailed. Though several off-world races have intermingled with our DNA, a secret key laid untouched within us. No wonder the Elohim have visited Earth periodically. They were checking in on their favorite experiment," I said, chuckling. "I now understand why the Angelic Realm has exhorted spiritual groups to help turn around our own tendency toward self-destruction. The Angelic Realm has to remind us of the hidden greatness within us to get us to overcome our own self-hatred and our blatant, collective death wish. Against all odds, we somehow persevered by choosing to remember who we truly are—just in time to anchor Timeline Three in place of Timeline One and Timeline Two."

"The ancient Gnostics must have known about this secret key," commented Lazarus. "For in one of their manuscripts, found in the Nag Hammadi collection, called 'The Apocryphon of John,' there is a metaphor for what the Elohim have unleashed on all the galactic races through the creation of humanity. In the manuscript there exist two opposing forces. The protagonist is Barbelo, the highest form of Wisdom. She even stands above the archetypal Divine Feminine found in the ancient religions. In Gnostic Christian writing, it says of her, 'Before all else was I made known.' A statement like that literally places her before all of creation. The other force is the Archon, what some might consider evil personified, who decides to blind humanity from knowing its greatness through what are called the five veils of forgetfulness. The Archon stood jealously against humanity. In the manuscript, the Barbelo decides to keep a secret from Yahweh, the Creator, by putting a secret seed within the depths of the human soul. Then, when the time came for humanity to fall into the pit of self-destruction because of the five veils, the seed sprouted forth. Finally, the Creator demanded to know how this had happened, and that's when the Barbelo revealed her secret—the name of the seed is Christ Consciousness."

"Things have certainly changed a lot for me since I've had these regressions with Leo," I said admiringly. "The information that came out of those sessions helped put things in perspective for me. For instance, my realization that my first abduction had involved the Elohim disguised as the Possum People changed everything for me. I now saw where all the breadcrumbs were leading, and why my story, my purpose, was no longer my story and my purpose. No longer do I feel like I have been observed under an ET microscope. The entire journey I have walked is no longer about me. There is a much bigger story: this is about humanity. The Divine Eye has been observing humanity under a cosmic microscope. I think that the Elohim have pulled off the same stunt that the Barbelo pulled. I found myself flooded by numerous insights while watching the videos of my sessions."

"Are you aware of your ancestors' prophecy of the Elohim?" asked Lazarus.

Remembering that I was of Cree lineage, I assumed that it might have something to do with that. "Is it a Cree prophecy?"

"Yes, it is. You might've heard it being called the Prophecy of the Rainbow Warriors."

"I guess I've heard of it. But what does Elohim have to do with it?"

"According to legend, the prophecy originated with an old wise woman of the Cree Nation, named Eyes of Fire. She had been given a vision of the future, when the day would come that the greed that led to the ravaging of the Earth, the devastation of the forests, the blackening of the waters, the falling of birds from the air, and the poisoning of our rivers would come to an end. At this time the Rainbow Warriors would appear and restore everything to health.

"They would proclaim a day of awakening when all the tribes of the Earth would form a New World of justice, peace, freedom, and recognition of the Divine-in-All. These warriors would teach all the tribes the secrets of Unity, Love, and Understanding, secrets that would bring harmony to the four corners of the Earth and to all living things. Out of this harmony would emerge a new way of choosing our rulers. No longer would elections be based on those who spoke the most eloquent lies, but on those whose actions matched their speeches. The people would become a new people, whose hearts would radiate love, blessing all with mutual respect."

The waitress approached and asked if we would like an English style sundowner for the evening.

"The way I feel, I'm not sure I should be drinking anything other than tea," I said.

"For a person who likes to live dangerously," Lazarus winked, "you sure play it safe."

"I think he's in the mood for more than tea," said the waitress. "I know just the thing."

Sitting next to one of the arched windows, flanked by antique gas lights fed long ago by gas instead of electricity lines, we took in the immensity of the Cascade Bar's unique copper-tiled ceiling. The stateliness of the carved wood and the luxurious floral-patterned green carpet contrasted handsomely with the richness of the copper. For 102 years this landmark has entertained royalty and aristocrats alongside skiers and tourists. After our drinks arrived, Lazarus started staring me down.

"What...?" I asked, defensively.

"So, you didn't truthfully know about the Cree prophecy of the Elohim, even though you are part Cree?"

"No. My interest in my ancestral heritage has mostly been in the musical vein. I've read that the Cree believe there are several means to attain spirit, a few being speaking through visions and dreams. I seem to have inherited the gift of the dreamer. But I also have this innate ability to use music, especially the flute, to bring a wonderful calm to people young and old. I feel guided as I'm playing. From what I understand, the idea of spirits working through us is a deep root of Cree spirituality. In similar fashion, the Cree have strong beliefs regarding their ancestors, what little I have learned of mine. And yet there is some deep ancestral message that has always called to me. I have yet to completely understand it. Maybe because there is a conflict with my Czech side. I'm not sure."

"That has nothing to do with it," said Lazarus. "However, I do know that the Cree also have a very strong belief that neither the spirits nor the people ever depart fully."

I replied, "That's what was so eerie about the being that called itself Elohim. I felt such unmistakable ancestral connection to it. It really shook me," I told him.

"Stan, do you know anything about the Elohim?"

"Only what I have learned from my regression and from you."

"Well, let me give you a little background. The Elohim show up in more than one religion. The most documented version comes out of the Judeo-Christian writings. From the Hebrew tradition, *Elohim* is one of the names of God. It is one of the rare instances when God is referred to in the plural, just like this being that approached you as 'we.' There is a very strange passage in Scripture that states, 'The Sons of God slept with the daughters of men.' Sons of God are actually a translation of Bene Elohim. The implication is that the Elohim somehow had influence on the genetic makeup of humanity. In various writings throughout the world, they show up periodically to check up on their progeny, like some lab experiment. In Egyptian writings, they are called the Ptah, and in esoteric writings the Paa Tal—loosely translated it means 'The First Breath' or 'The First People,' a term used by many Native People. No matter which way you choose to look at it, or which tradition you choose to employ, the bottom line seems to be that humans are closely related to these creator beings. And, again, I believe their secret to be stored in our human DNA."

"I'm still not too sure about this," I teased.

"There are several documented digs where giant skeletons have been dug up, somewhere between ten feet and thirty-five feet tall. In Scripture, it says that these giants had a name. They were called 'Nephilim.' In Scripture, in the Book of Genesis, it says, 'There were giants on the earth in those days; and also after that, when the sons of God, the Bene Elohim, came in unto the daughters of men, and they bared children to them, the same became mighty men which were of old, men of renown.' I paraphrased it, but that's the gist."

"So, you're a mystic and a scholar."

"I won't go into the many writings about the Nephilim because it will only add to the complexity of what your story suggests. Your sessions reveal that your role in life has deeply profound implications."

Mixed emotions surged within me. Lazarus's words were beginning to scare me. I wasn't sure I wanted to hear any more.

In vain, I sucked on my Long Island Iced Tea as if it were a source of comfort.

"Here is what is so troubling to me," Lazarus continued. "I personally believe there are no coincidences. At this very time, you have two conjoining realities over which the world may possibly hang you up by your heels. You have these hybrid children showing up at the same time that the Elohim are appearing. To me, this is a return of the ancient stories. And I am disturbed by the significance."

"What are you trying to tell me?"

"Scripture makes no bones about the fact that the Elohim somehow messed with the DNA of humanity. Over the course of human history, DNA continued to be altered in various ways by different species. In some cases, DNA strands were disconnected to dummy us down, leaving us with the remnants that our science calls 'junk DNA.' In other instances, our enduring these blatant manipulations of our genes somehow made us stronger—the ultimate survivor. It seems that we have become the ultimate hybrid.

"One contactee, Alex Collier, claims that he received from the Andromedans that humanity has the DNA of twenty-two different humanoid species. Other contactees speak of even more non-Earth genes in our DNA. How we verify such information is beyond me. But the point is that this planet is a melting pot of different races. And our DNA is apparently unique in special ways."

"It sort of reminds me of the ideas uncovered by the hypnotist Dolores Cannon."

"I've read all her works. In one of them, she discovered a choice piece of information. She managed to get access to the Greys through hypnosis of an abductee. In the hypnosis session, a Grey told Cannon that the Greys consider human DNA to be 'royal DNA.' It's one of the reasons they are using humans to try and save their own race, which is in the process of going extinct. Though I can't prove this right now, I suspect that this royal DNA is somehow linked to the Elohim.

"It's true that the Nephilim, or the Bene Elohim, had a terrible role in making slaves out of humanity—taking control for millennia through ruling classes that operated as their minions. I will tell you here and now, Stan, this will not be allowed to ever happen again. What I am telling you is that you really have to make a decision about what is happening around you right now. Are you a pawn or are you the voice of the New Man, the Elohim? Since you've been visited by the Elohim, you are going to have to find out why they are here. Are we about to enter into the Golden Age of Enlightenment, as foretold by your Cree ancestors, or are we about to be fooled into thinking we have reached a pinnacle only to be manipulated once again?"

I sat there feeling as if the ceiling of the magnificent Stanley Hotel was crumbling down on me. Either Lazarus was a raving madman, or he was making me out to be one. Either way, I didn't like it.

"Now it seems like you are purposely trying to freak me out here, Lazarus. I came here to clarify my answers. And honestly, all you are doing is leaving me with more questions. Now I'm even more confused."

"Stan, in the Timeline Wars, I spoke of the Looking Glass Project. Do remember my trying to explain that to you?"

"Yeah. But all it did was make me crazy."

"Well, what I did not tell you was that part of the information, from the three whistleblowers of the Looking Glass Project, had to do with the Elohim. They said precious little about the Elohim, but what they did reveal was that the Elohim have been at war with the Dracos, who some call the Reptilians, for millions of years. It was a horrendous period of time when war enveloped Orion from one corner to the other. The information from the Looking Glass Project and another top-secret project said that the two most ancient races in our galaxy are the Dracos and the Elohim. And both are considered the most pure of all races. It's like a scientific version of Satan versus the angels. Only the Elohim are nothing to mess with. They are an extremely high order of being. That's why they show up in religious traditions as gods. Yet why are they engaged in something as low as war? To me, it can only mean one thing: That we are talking about the fight for the very soul of humanity. And what is so disturbing to me is that this fight seems to have landed on your doorstep. From your sessions, it appears that the Elohim have returned to the Earth. Have they brought war or are they about to bring forth a secret millions of years in the making?"

"And what do you make of my hybrid daughters? Why are they so skittish? Why do they appear only to quickly disappear? Why don't they simply talk to me?" I asked.

"I have said nothing to you about your hybrid daughters. But I do have information from sources that say the Black Ops have been working with the 'dark ones,' let's call them, and are attempting to kill every single one of them. What has strong implications is that these girls represent some dynamic that can mean the Elohim have revisited the Earth either to bring an end to galactic war, or to reveal a long-held secret as to why they became involved with humanity in the first place. Even both. It can only mean that this is no small matter. And this visit that you have had with them leaves me with grave concern. I say again that we must be talking about a battle for the soul of humanity."

"Lazarus, I came here hoping you could throw some light on the truth. And all you've done is totally confuse me. Look at me," I said with a smirk on my face, "I'm shaking."

All kidding aside I really was shaking. What Lazarus had said was unbelievable, but I somehow knew there was truth in his words.

"I'm sorry, Stan. But I believe your confusion comes from wanting to stay in denial rather than trying to understand the truth. You know who you are. You saw that when the Rainbow Spirit showed up. You saw your past; you saw the truth around your own soul. You saw your purpose. You know that. Now you have the Elohim showing up. How can I tell you what you want when you don't even want to believe what you already know? There is nothing more I can tell you as to why these beings have shown up. If this tall blue-white thing shows up again, please, ask as many questions as you possibly can. We have to find out whether we are looking at a seminal event with the forces of Heaven, or whether we are being manipulated once again to prevent the Cree prophecy from coming true."

I sat there feeling as if the fiery breath of a dragon had singed me. Then, as if on cue, I had a flash of sudden knowingness. Despite all the chaos and conflict, despite the persistent dark deeds of the Illuminati to collapse the economies of the world and stir up odium and war, and despite the apathy that consumed most of humanity, enough people were finally waking up to remember their true divine nature. In the end, good would triumph over evil, wisdom over ignorance, and love over hatred. I mean, it had to, right?

I looked up to see that Lazarus was watching me keenly. He smiled, as if he sensed the tone of my positive thoughts. "You are a True Orion soul. You are in service and you are here to help," he said affirmatively. "The great gathering has begun and no one is to be left out of this circle. There must be a unity of man before humans understand who they truly are. You are a messenger."

With that same sudden knowingness I reluctantly understood everything. Tears began to run down my face, "And the message will get through to the people," I said, raising my glass to offer a toast. Our glasses clinked symbolically, like the final note of triumph in the song of the universe.

We finished our drinks, shared warm words, and eventually it was time to go. I walked Lazarus to the front lobby of the hotel to say our final goodbyes, and, after gathering up enough courage, I turned to ask him, "John, who are you, really?"

"Give me a last hug, Stan." As we shared a final embrace, he whispered, "We are here to guide." Stepping back he gave me a slap on the back as he winked, smiled, and walked away, out the doors and through the parking lot, never to be seen again.

Goosebumps ran the length of my body. I stood alone on the steps of the Stanley Hotel, dazed by the realization that I, again, had an amazing visitation with a friend in disguise.

The End...

Epilogue
The End—A New Beginning

We woke up this morning to another beautiful day. When we went to bed last night, it was the end...the end of the day, the end of an argument and the end of...nothing. Everything in life revolves around this concept: What we perceive to be the end is actually the beginning. We have all been given a gift of great tomorrows, of new beginnings. And just as the Third Timeline suggests, the possibilities are endless. We are the creators of our tomorrows—our own destiny.

Although I know that my role as a messenger is important, I must confess that I didn't fully grasp the big picture. Now I do. I look forward to making a difference in the world. I will share my message and, in doing so, my tomorrows will be filled with love, humor, understanding, compassion, and knowledge. I will touch the lives of many, and many will hear what I have to share, while others won't.

On some level I can appreciate that there are humans who disagree with me, even to the point of repeatedly threatening my life. The Black Ops, I'm sure, believe they are doing the right thing. I will send them good thoughts, and not allow that to sully my life. Life is about diversity. Life is even more about love and the harmony that results when different notes are played together. Is it too outrageous to expect others to recognize that I am an honorable man, wishing to bring forward a better world? But more than that—a better universe?

I am not a teacher; I am not a preacher. I am a messenger, simply telling my story. I do not stand here assuming that great wonders will come through me. I stand here awash in knowing that I am a grain of sand, indicating that a new world is in the making, made up of millions of other grains of sand foretelling of a shore that bridges sea and land to a world far beyond anything we may presume to know.

As a member of the human race, you have within you the ability to change quantum reality naturally. In short, you can manifest what you believe! More than that, humans have a direct connection to source; some call it the Oneness, or God. In any case it is an unimagined consciousness. Humans just need to learn that they have this ability, a natural gift, from the Great Spirit itself, God.

As Lisa said, "We are the ones we have been waiting for." We are the oneness. Together we can make a difference. We can create the outcome of this new timeline—the Third Timeline. Together we are already moving into global enlightenment and a possible paradise on earth. If things continue on their current path, it will be a culmination of ancient prophecies of a Golden Age, a spiritual and intellectual renaissance for humanity unlike anything previously known in recorded history. The "We" includes humans and all other sentient beings through the Universe. Whether we're fully conscious of it or not, we are all working together to guide humanity to fully manifesting Timeline Three.

The shift has begun, and if everyone rises to the occasion and things go the way I believe they will, 2012 will prove to be an amazing time in history, a new beginning. But first, the message must be delivered. And each of you then becomes the messenger. The more people who can understand that we are not alone, and the more people who can tune in to the vibration of love, the more likely we are to experience a shift into global enlightenment; and the less likely we are to experience the dreary reality of greed, and the incessant outbreaks of war and hatred.

I have fulfilled this part of my mission. I have shared the information. It is now up to each of you to share it with others, to join me as messengers of hope and understanding. Be fearless. Own your power, your birthright from God, by choosing love, peace, and compassion for all living beings.

The beginning...

About the Author

Stan Romanek's hypnotic regressions, transcribed in this book, provide a dramatic explanation of why some of the ETs are here, their goals and purposes, and the far-reaching changes on the Earth we may expect in the near future. The equations Stan received during sleep and hypnosis suggest the involvement of an advanced ET intelligence. They have deep physical meaning and convey new ideas far beyond Stan's ability to fabricate. The regressions provided the chance to interact directly with this intelligence, to pose questions and receive answers.

The Orion Regressions is a full transcription of five regression sessions conducted by Dr. R. Leo Sprinkle that explore Stan's contact with extraterrestrial beings. Although Stan's first book, international bestseller *Messages: The World's Most Documented Extraterrestrial Contact Story* talks about his experiences, it also sets the stage for things to come that would lead up to *The Orion Regressions*. Unlike most regression sessions, something extraordinary happened, and it would become apparent that a consciousness other than Stan's was using his body to communicate. *The Orion Regressions* is a companion book to Stan's follow-up book, *Answers: The World's Most Documented Extraterrestrial Contact Story Continues*, and contains messages given through Stan by beings claiming to be True Orions. These beings brought forth a wealth of information vital to humanity.

Visit the author on-line at www.stanromanek.com
and on Facebook at fb.com/StanRomanek

Printed in Great Britain
by Amazon.co.uk, Ltd.,
Marston Gate.